TERENCE CONRAN
KITCHENS
THE HUB OF THE HOME

conran
OCTOPUS

DEDICATION This book is for Vicki, who has made the kitchen the happy hub of our home and cooks many wonderful meals for our friends, family, chefs and even Conran Shop buyers and directors.

8 Introduction

16 Planning and Design

60 Kitchen Living

116 Basic Elements

170 Fittings and Appliances

208 Resources

216 Suppliers

220 Index

223 Acknowledgements

INTRODUCTION

What do you do in your kitchen? More to the point, what don't you do? These days, the kitchen's role extends far beyond its original, central function as the place where food is stored, prepared and cooked. Increasingly it doubles up as an eating area, home office, playroom, entertainment zone, chatroom and domestic nerve centre, and much else besides. In many households today, the kitchen forms the backdrop for a large part of what constitutes everyday living.

If one were to plot a day in the life of the average kitchen at the beginning of the twenty-first century, one might well record a constant stream of activity: preparing for the day at work or school...paying bills, writing lists and carrying out other routine administrative chores...children playing under a parent's watchful eye or tackling homework at the kitchen table...socialising with friends...washing, drying and ironing clothes...watching TV and listening to music...making phone calls and taking messages...having a quiet drink and swapping news at the end of the day...and all this in addition to making meals (and in many cases, sitting down to eat them).

The idea of the kitchen as fully fledged living space is relatively new. When I was working on my first *Kitchen Book*, twenty-five years ago, we included the New York kitchen of George Lang, the celebrated Hungarian restaurateur and owner of Café des Artistes. The all-embracing nature of his kitchen, with its sound systems, television, office area and wine storage, was fairly unusual for its time; today, such inclusiveness is far more expected. In my own kitchen in the country, there's a small table set aside where children can indulge in some of their messier creative pursuits; there's a television, but also an open fire. In my apartment in London, the whole of the upper floor is an open-plan kitchen/dining/living space: whoever's doing the cooking can watch TV across the room if they want, or talk to people while they prepare a meal.

Filled with light and air, this open kitchen, dining and living area reflects the informality of contemporary lifestyles in its free arrangement of space. The L-shaped layout of cooking and preparation areas maximises floor space and offers a neat way of integrating fixtures and appliances.

What is it about the kitchen that makes it attract roles with an almost centrifugal force? One answer must have something to do with the kitchen's fundamental association with food. A lot of the time we may eat to live, rather than live to eat, but the enjoyment of food goes beyond satisfying the basic need to keep body and soul together. Good food, particularly good food eaten in company, promotes a deep sense of well-being; it's simply one of life's greatest pleasures.

Statistics may show that we spend less time cooking today than ever before: in Britain, the amount of time professional working people spend cooking for pleasure in the average week is supposedly down to only 1.8 hours. But given the central importance of food in our lives, both physically and emotionally, perhaps it is not surprising that we're choosing to spend more of our time in the nurturing environment of the kitchen, even if that time is spent doing things other than cooking.

In a similar way, when so much of contemporary life is mediated via television or computer screens, part of the kitchen's appeal is that it can offer a means of grounding yourself in reality, a touchstone of tastes, smells and textures that serves as an antidote

PREVIOUS PAGES: The enjoyment of food – and shared mealtimes – is one of the great pleasures of life. **BELOW:** Vernacular styles of kitchen decoration and fitting still hold tremendous appeal, due to nostalgic associations with kitchens we might have known as children. **BELOW RIGHT:** A more recent kitchen role model is the professional- or catering-style kitchen, which relies heavily on stainless steel fittings, appliances and surfaces.

to 'virtual' experience. If the idea of the kitchen as a 'reality' zone seems far-fetched, one has only to scan a shelf of bestselling cookbooks to see how often 'real' comes up in the title. Indeed, many of today's most successful cookbooks and most popular cooking programmes are far less to do with ingredients and recipes than they are celebrations of sensuality and appetite. Kitchens, in this sense, are not promoted as places where, of necessity, we *have* to be; they're places where we *want* to be.

Pressure on time may also help to account for the kitchen's new inclusiveness. When time is short, people are less inclined to stand on ceremony. The old notion of the kitchen as the 'downstairs' domain of the cook and her kitchenmaids, only visited with some trepidation by the mistress of the house, disappeared along with the servant class well over half a century ago. For a while, when kitchens became the housewife's exclusive realm, the distinction between the 'working' parts of the home and those areas where guests were welcomed and entertained remained in place. But as more and more women have gone out to work and the average household has shrunk to variations on the theme of the family unit, kitchens have necessarily emerged from behind the scenes. If the time

you are spending cooking means less time for relaxing, entertaining and simply being with your family – then the idea of closeting yourself behind closed doors to prepare a meal can be very unappealing. Nor does anyone particularly want to rush home from work and shut themselves away to fret anxiously over ingredients and cooking times while everyone is having a good time somewhere else.

As the kitchen has absorbed roles, it has also inevitably redefined the way we use space. A kitchen that could comfortably accommodate at least some of the roles sketched out above is necessarily on the large side. But at the same time, space is increasingly at a premium these days and many people find themselves settling for homes that are smaller than they would like. The solution to this apparent dilemma has inevitably involved a little creative interior shape-shifting. As more of what comprises everyday living has migrated into the kitchen, the kitchen has encroached first on the dining room and secondly on living areas in general. 'Kitchen-diners' have long been a common planning arrangement in many homes; today, however, the development of this concept has led to the single multi-purpose space that embraces a range of activities from relaxing and eating to cooking and working.

BELOW LEFT: Kitchens are the hardest-working areas in the home and consequently demand precision planning. Sound planning becomes even more critical when available space is tight. This kitchen, fitted along the length of a wall, doubles up as a spatial divider.

BELOW RIGHT: The sleek seamless fitting of this compact kitchen area, integrated into a narrow corridor immediately off a workspace, is the ultimate in reticence.

ABOVE: The kitchen as sleek workbench makes an almost sculptural statement in a loft space. Such modular designs, which liberate kitchen planning from walls and partitions, are increasingly popular. This 'kitchen cube' incorporates oven, fridge, dishwasher, hob and sink in a single unit; the stainless steel top can be slid across to serve as a table or additional preparation space.

In this sense, one might almost say that the 'kitchen' as a separate, isolated entity has disappeared, shrunk to a functional zone within a space where activities flow freely from one area to the next.

One impetus for this change has arisen with the vogue for 'loft living', even when the 'loft' is little more than an average-sized apartment. Open-plan kitchen-living-dining areas have long been popular in the United States, particularly on the West Coast, but rather more surprising is the fact that an estimated 20 per cent of new properties in London now feature open-plan kitchen designs, a sizable proportion given the traditionally conservative nature of Britain's property developers and house-builders.

In the more literal sense, kitchens in some cities are disappearing altogether. Many New York apartments designed for professionals omit any kitchen facilities at all, on the assumption that childless affluent singles prefer to eat out all the time, a trend aided and abetted by the fact that restaurant-going plays a central role in many people's social lives. I can sympathise with those who wish to simplify their lives to such an extent and I can appreciate that in dense metropolitan areas like New York it makes sense to maximise space, but I personally would find it very difficult to distinguish between an apartment without a kitchen and a hotel room. Much as I enjoy hotels, I wouldn't want to live in one.

For me and I suspect many people, kitchens indeed are the hub of the home. I would also argue that they are the heart of family life. A kitchen that is big enough to live in and eat in prevents families from fragmenting into a collection of individuals who eat their ready-prepared meals alone in front of the television (with many households owning more than one set, it may not even be the same television). The kitchen is one of the few remaining places where families can be guaranteed to spend at least some time together; where children can learn how to eat, what to eat and (hopefully) how to behave; where a little of the ceremony and ritual of shared mealtimes can be enacted.

Only a few decades ago, the 'dream' kitchens of popular imagination were chiefly defined in terms of their 'style' or the sophistication with which they were equipped. In the 1950s and early 1960s, the kitchens that everyone wanted were dazzling models of efficiency, with their wipe-clean surfaces, fitted units and new domestic appliances. By the 1970s country kitchens were the height of fashion, featuring warm, woody surfaces – we sold plenty of them at Habitat – mutating into the more self-consciously nostalgic or period looks of the 1980s. Then, inspired by the restaurant boom and the rise in eating out as a social activity, wannabe professional-style kitchens, all in gleaming stainless steel, became status symbols of the last decade.

Today, however, I suspect that dream kitchens are visualised very differently. On the basis of some very unscientific research, it appears that what people want is a kitchen that suits the way they want to live. 'Big and bright', 'somewhere large enough to live in and entertain in', 'a big table to eat on and work on', 'a back door open to the garden', 'everything to hand', 'not too neat – Post-it notes (stickies) or magnets on the fridge' were some of the answers from this informal survey. The picture that emerges is not a kitchen lifted straight from a manufacturer's brochure, but a simple, calm and welcoming place at the heart of the home.

This new emphasis on kitchen living does not mean you can neglect the kitchen's prime function. For kitchens to be enjoyable and pleasant places, they must, first of all, work well, which means integrating servicing with the layout of appliances, providing enough storage space and areas for preparation, getting the lighting right and a host of other practical considerations. Once these basic elements have been properly considered, everything else is more likely to fall into place.

In many ways, life is overcomplicated these days. The kitchen should be one place where we remember to keep it simple.

ABOVE LEFT: This kitchen suspended from the underside of a mezzanine represents a rather unusual way of maximising floor space and providing uninterrupted views, a service core literally at the heart of the home. Sliding panels screen working areas when not in use. **ABOVE RIGHT:** Borrowing heavily from the science lab, these plug-in gas rings on their tiled base provide a cooking set-up that offers optimum flexibility. The design is a prototype.

Planning
and Design

The kitchen is the most intensively used space in the home and the one place where we are spending more and more time. Thoughtful planning and careful design is therefore essential before you undertake any alteration or purchase any new equipment.

A well-designed kitchen will allow you to move smoothly from task to task in a logical sequence and to work comfortably, safely and efficiently. It will also allow you to integrate a wide variety of appliances and equipment seamlessly into your living space. The key is to create a blueprint which incorporates every requirement for you and your circumstances, while allowing flexibility for future change.

BELOW: Everyday cooking utensils and basic ingredients can be as effective as a display of artfully arranged objects, and this way, the most regularly used items are also within easy reach of the cook. **RIGHT:** Architectural features are a good starting point for kitchen design. This kitchen retains a strong sense of character and individuality that is enhanced by the laboratory-style workbench. **FAR RIGHT:** A split-level island unit makes sound ergonomic sense. The lower section is used for cooking and preparing food while guests can perch on bar stools at the higher level.

The basics of good planning are the same whether you want to change your kitchen dramatically – a rip-it-out-and-start-again project with new units, appliances, flooring, worktops and so on – or if you just fancy an update or cosmetic improvements. Both require financial commitment and a period of planning if you are to achieve the optimum design. To reach the definitive layout, you need to review all the options, taking into account space, function and budget.

If you decide to seek professional advice from an architect or a kitchen designer, you will still need to have a firm idea of what you want from your kitchen and what decorative style you prefer. Good research and thorough preparation are therefore indispensable. That's not to say you shouldn't follow your creative instincts, but hasty decisions can often lead to expensive mistakes.

A good design will create a good-looking kitchen tailormade to your way of working. It will also save money by helping you to allocate your budget effectively. Consider all the options and the benefits will be long lasting – a stylish and practical kitchen that you will enjoy for years to come.

ADDING VALUE

A good kitchen is often at the top of a potential homebuyer's wish list, after location and price. In fact, installing a new kitchen is almost guaranteed to add value to the property, more so than any other home improvement, and will also help to sell the house more quickly. However, it is important to reconcile the cost of improvements with the resale value it adds. If you plan to move on in a few years, think carefully about expenditure; although a kitchen does add value to your home, it is rarely equivalent to the cost of the kitchen. The amount you spend must also relate to the value of the property and you are unlikely to recoup your money if you put a top-of-the-range kitchen into a small, terraced house.

The most important consideration is that you choose a kitchen you will enjoy using. However, it is wise to make changes that reflect mainstream taste now that a kitchen has become such a selling point – your successors may not be as enamoured with a bubblegum-pink kitchen as you are, though paint colours are easy to change. Choose neutral shades and classic-style cupboards rather than quirky fittings and state-of-the-art appliances. Plan the kitchen so that it is not so idiosyncratic that someone else can't use it. That said, making a kitchen nondescript is also inadvisable, so if you live in an older home, try to retain the character and period details such as original glass cupboards, picture mouldings and timber worktops which often end up as financial as well as aesthetic assets.

You may want to update your current kitchen rather than shoulder the cost of a full refit. A solid, well-organised kitchen inherited from a previous owner can be improved by simple, cosmetic changes such as painting cupboard doors or filling open shelving with your own collection of china. Replacing tiles, worktops and new cupboard door

handles can also transform a tired-looking kitchen for little outlay and is an effective way of personalising the room. You could also improve your kitchen layout and storage capacity by moving a radiator, the sink or the location of your existing appliances.

PLANNING FROM SCRATCH

The most crucial question to consider is whether the kitchen is in the right place. For instance, it may make sense to move the kitchen from the ground floor to the basement so that it leads onto the garden, thus making it easier to transfer food for outdoor dining and barbecues and hang laundry on a washing line. You can also keep an eye on young children playing outside while preparing meals. Alternatively, moving the kitchen to the top floor may offer better light and space, while bedrooms may benefit from being relocated to a cool basement. Design the layout of your house around how you live – if the kitchen is the centre of your home, reshuffle the rooms accordingly, so the kitchen gets the best location and optimum natural light.

If you are fortunate enough to be able to choose which direction your kitchen will face, in a new-build house or a total refurbishment, it is a good idea to orientate it towards the sunrise. This will flood the room with morning light, and give you an opportunity to utilise the solar energy.

Even if you don't relocate the kitchen to another room, you may want to restructure the space by removing or moving walls, windows or doors. If you are considering any structural alterations, always seek professional advice.

Whether your kitchen is a separate room or an open-plan, inclusive layout, it should blend smoothly with entrances, halls and staircases. If the kitchen leads onto the garden, you may consider adding a back-door porch or lobby to keep coats, umbrellas and shoes out and the heat in or build on an extra larder if north-facing. And if your kitchen is the main 'corridor' from the entrance of the house to the back garden and doubles up as a busy thoroughfare, it may be wise to add another back exit elsewhere. If this is impossible, make sure the primary work area is sited away

LEFT: A huge, weathered table is the focus of family activity and the inspiration for this rustic kitchen. The kitchen units neatly screen off the utility area and are coated with blackboard paint, while the black rubber flooring injects a hint of metropolitan style into the otherwise simple scheme.

from the two doors and out of the way of passing traffic. Professional advice will often cast a fresh perspective on space and location.

When it comes to kitchen planning, bigger isn't necessarily better. Layout is more important than size and large kitchens are only practical if the appliances and storage units are ergonomically arranged. A smaller kitchen does not mean compromising on function or sacrificing style. And in practical terms, a smaller surface area means you will spend less on materials and so afford better-quality ones.

Permissions

If you intend to add a room or alter any part of the front elevation (particularly if you live in a conservation area), you will usually require planning permission. It is a good idea to contact the planning department at a very early stage, even before commissioning any drawings or plans. They can indicate what is acceptable and what is not, and, in most cases, advise whether planning permission is required, saving you time and possibly money.

If you intend to convert a disused basement into a kitchen, you may have to notify the planning authorities of a change of use. And if you live in a listed building, you will require listed building consent for any alteration that affects its character or setting. Any structural alterations – for example, putting a door in a structural wall or removing a chimney breast – will require building regulations approval, even if you do not need planning permission. If you hire an architect or interior designer, it is their responsibility to seek such permission. If you do the work yourself, start with the building inspector and ask to be referred to any other organisation whose permission is required.

ABOVE: A chrome kettle and toaster are the only signs of ornamentation in this open-plan kitchen, which is part of a loft apartment in a 1920s warehouse conversion. A simple bar separates the kitchen from the dining area. **RIGHT:** The well-planned kitchen ensures the cook has everything to hand. Here, a seemingly effortless mix of unfitted units, freestanding appliances and open shelving belies the meticulous planning and organisation that has gone into the design.

WORKING OUT PRIORITIES

Before you start planning you need to determine your priorities and anticipate future needs. By looking at your style of life, the architecture of your house and your cooking habits, you will gradually build up an idea of the style and design of kitchen you want. Then ask yourself whether you would you feel happier handing the project, either partly or fully, over to a professional.

Function

▸ How regularly is your kitchen used?

▸ What activities will you do there: food preparation and cooking; food storage; everyday eating; entertaining; laundry; office and schoolwork; watching television?

▸ Who uses the kitchen? Are you a single person, a professional couple without children or part of a large family?

▸ Do you want a designated eating area, whether it's a table, a breakfast bar or island unit?

▸ Are you a serious cook or do you feed yourself from tins, packets and pre-prepared food?

▸ Do you keep pets who eat or sleep in the room?

▸ Can the kitchen be comfortably used, or adapted for use, by a less-able or elderly person?

Space

▸ Look at the size and shape of your kitchen. Is it big enough for the activities, appliances and storage you require, without restricting movement? If not, is it feasible to enlarge the space or add an extension, taking into account your budget and timescale?

RIGHT: The kitchen is the multifunctional hub of the home, a place where meals can be eaten and children can play without interrupting the kitchen's primary function – cooking – a shift marked here by the change in flooring.

FAR RIGHT: Natural light is a key feature of the kitchen. This dark space has been opened up with a large skylight, which lets daylight flood in. White cupboard fronts, pale flooring and a painted ceiling bounce the light into dark corners.

▸ How many doors are there? Do they open in or out? Are they correctly placed or could any be repositioned to better advantage?

▸ Can you design a new kitchen without undermining the original character of your home? Have you considered the architectural features in the room such as pillars or chimney breasts?

▸ Consider the aspect of the room and its scale.

▸ How much natural light is there in the room? If there is little or none, consider ways of obtaining or increasing the amount of daylight with a roof skylight, patio doors or full-length windows.

▸ Is there access to an outside wall for ducting?

▸ Can it be naturally ventilated?

Needs

▸ List what you like and dislike about your existing kitchen, then list the qualities for your ideal kitchen. Evaluate what is an essential improvement and what you can do without.

▸ What are your priorities: a view from your kitchen window; more light; plenty of worktop space and storage; a family-friendly room; direct access to outside areas?

▸ What are your favourite kitchen styles? Start a kitchen design file for your ideas and start collecting brochures, magazine cuttings, samples of tiles, flooring, and paint colours that you like.

▸ Which kitchen appliances do you want? Built-in or freestanding oven; refrigerator and freezer; dishwasher; microwave; waste disposal unit? Could laundry appliances be moved elsewhere to free up more space?

▸ Make a list of all your small appliances to help you decide how many sockets you will need and where they should go. Evaluate whether you actually use all of them and how often. Infrequently used appliances could be stored out of the kitchen if storage space is limited.

▸ How much storage space will you require for dried goods, pots and pans, small appliances; wine; cutlery and china? Do you want any or all items on display, everything tucked away in cupboards or a combination of both?

Safety

Most accidents at home involve children and kitchens, so try to incorporate these planning precautions.

▸ Install cookers and hobs away from windows – draughts may extinguish gas flames and curtains may catch alight. Gas hobs with a flame-failure device will cut off the supply if the flame is accidentally extinguished.

▸ Choose a non-slip material for floors.

▸ Place heavy items such as casserole dishes and small appliances in the base cupboards or shelves. Lighter items like glassware and packets can be stored in wall units while deep drawers with non-slip bases allow crockery to be stored without sliding as the drawer is opened and closed.

▸ If paint was applied to a surface in your kitchen before 1980, there is a 50 per cent chance it contains lead. There are kits available from DIY stores if you want to check.

▸ Flexes on small appliances should be shortened or replaced with curly ones to prevent children pulling on any flex which might overhang the worktop. Never trail flexes across a sink or hob or install electrical switches and power points near a water source.

▸ Flank cooking areas with a heat-resistant worktop.

▸ Choose rounded or axis corners on worktops.

▸ Ensure work surfaces and cooking areas are well lit.

▸ Fit child locks on any drawers and doors containing chemicals or other potentially dangerous objects. All kitchens should contain a fire extinguisher and fire blanket.

▸ If you do any deep-fat frying, learn how to put out a fat fire (i.e. smother the flames with a damp cloth).

ERGONOMICS

When it comes to planning your kitchen, ergonomics is a key consideration. The most important rule here is the 'work triangle', a concept worked out by ergonomic studies in the early 1950s (and based on research conducted in the 1920s to improve industrial efficiency). These studies showed that the overall distance between your sink, fridge and cooker – the three chief activity centres in the kitchen – should not be too great. Since nearly all the manual labour done in the kitchen involves laps between the three, the objective is to make the distances between them comfortable. The study established carefully measured distances between these three primary kitchen areas to optimise convenience and safety. Ideally, an imaginary line joining the sink, fridge and cooker should measure no more than 6m in total, although the sides of the triangle can vary according to the size and shape of the room. However, the distance between each work zone should be at least 900mm. If the distances are too far, you will waste energy moving from one end of the kitchen to the other. If the distances are too short, working in the kitchen becomes cramped and uncomfortable.

Divide your kitchen into sectors. Start with the food storage area, which should include the fridge and ideally cupboards and a work surface for preparation. Next is the cooking area, where the oven and hob should be flanked by worktops suitable for placing hot pans on. The sink area should also include nearby storage for crockery and cutlery after washing up.

The most important work space in the kitchen lies between the sink and the cooker, because that is where the most activity takes place. Situate the main food preparation area between the two – it should be the longest stretch of continuous worktop in the kitchen and large and durable

ABOVE LEFT: Tambour shutters create an 'appliance garage' for storing small electrical equipment, keeping long, trailing flexes out of reach.

RIGHT: Custom-made, floor-to-ceiling cupboards are kept away from the work triangle, but with the multi-depth wall units, maximise storage space.

LEFT: This kitchen incorporates a small curved peninsula to provide an extra work surface and a mini-breakfast bar where friends or family can be entertained while you cook.

ABOVE: The sleek functionality of this galley kitchen has been fully optimised with careful planning, light colours and plain, hardwearing materials like glass splashbacks.

enough to serve a meal. Neither the sink nor hob should be relegated to the corner of the room. Instead, place them at least 400mm from the corner so you can work over them without banging elbows or pans on the wall.

Basic rules

Depending on the size and shape of the kitchen, dimensions of the triangle will vary, but here are the basic concepts.
▶ Since plumbing is the most expensive item to change, start with the current position of the sink and plot the layout from there. Group laundry equipment and a dishwasher together and near the sink for easy plumbing.
▶ Place a worktop near the fridge so you can move food in and out quickly, reducing the amount of time the fridge door remains open.
▶ The cooker or hob should be placed along an exterior wall, making it easy to install an efficient ventilation system. Alternatively, if cooking appliances are fitted in a central island unit, install an overhead canopy hood.
▶ Avoid interrupting the flow of the work triangle with tall units or dressers. It is better to group tall units together at the end of a run of worktops in a fitted kitchen and in an area outside the triangle.
▶ Allow plenty of space for machine doors to open. Dishwasher doors and front-loading washing machines require more room because you have to stand in front or to the side of the door to fill and empty the machine.

Standard dimensions

The height of a kitchen is as important as the layout. Cupboards, shelves and drawers should be designed to minimise bending down and reaching up, especially for frequently used items and basic food supplies. Very wide, deep drawers below the work surface are ideal. These huge pull-outs – ranging from 90cm to 180cm wide – provide capacious storage and glide out smoothly with one pull.

It should not be assumed that the height of worktops must be completely uniform throughout your kitchen. Ideal working heights not only vary for different people but for different activities. The standard elbow-height of 90cm is recommended for general food preparation, but delicate, complex jobs, such as icing a cake, need a higher surface as you need to give closer attention. For heavier tasks such as kneading bread or rolling out pastry, where you need to put your full weight over the task, a lower level would be more convenient; say 75cm. The hob can also be lowered so you can see into the pans during cooking, stir easily and lift heavy pots off comfortably.

While it is a convenient advantage to have a worktop tailored to suit your height and the specific tasks you may carry out, worktops that vary too much in height can cause jarring visual disharmonies and can also overly complicate small kitchens, especially where there isn't much worktop space. Equally, tailoring your kitchen too much to one specific individual may restrict other users, including any future owner. It may be simpler and cheaper to build up the worktop with a thick slab of wood for chopping and use a tabletop with a marble slab for pastry making.

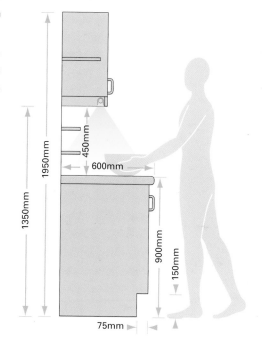

KITCHEN LAYOUTS

Don't be alarmed if your new kitchen is the size of a shoebox; efficient use of space depends more on how it is laid out, rather than how much there is. There are six basic layouts that, keeping within the work triangle, will create an efficient, practical kitchen.

The **SINGLE-LINE** kitchen is best utilised in narrow rooms and is suitable for one or two people to use at once. For this layout to work as an efficient kitchen, you ideally need 3m of uninterrupted wall space. Use built-in or built-under appliances to exploit all available space and allocate as much worktop as possible – the longest stretch should be between the oven and sink. Sliding cabinet doors may be more practical than hinged ones while extra storage can be provided by narrow glass shelves between the worktop and wall units. If it is part of an open-plan space, consider screening off the kitchen with sliding or folding doors, to contain cooking smells or hide dirty saucepans.

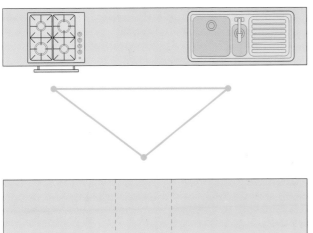

The **GALLEY** kitchen with two facing lines of cupboards provides the most efficient use of space, and is the layout most coveted by professional chefs. A galley is comprised of counters on both sides of the room with a corridor down the middle. There should be at least 1,200mm of space between facing units to allow comfortable access to base units; a pull-down table can be incorporated at one end. Try to add as much natural light as possible, especially if the kitchen is located in a dark or narrow corridor.

The **L-SHAPED** kitchen is a versatile layout with cupboards along two adjacent walls. It works well with a sitting area that is integrated into the same room and also overcomes any shortage of wall space. The hob, fridge and sink should ideally be separated by a length of worktop to provide adequate preparation space. Dead space in the corner can be maximised with a carousel or Magic Corner unit.

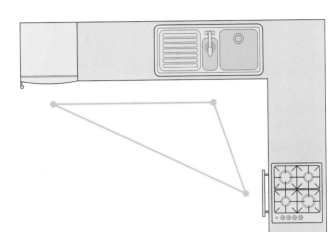

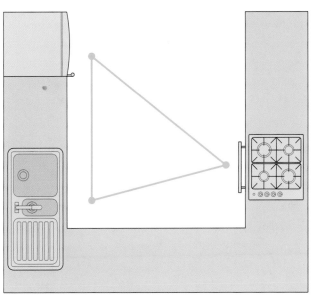

The **U-SHAPED** kitchen utilises three full walls of a room space. It is safe, efficient, offers maximum storage and work space and suits both large and small rooms. In a small kitchen, however, ensure there is at least 2m in the middle. The only weak point of a U-shaped plan is that separate work centres can become remote. To prevent this happening in long, thin rooms or very large kitchens, the work triangle should be restricted to the bottom of the U.

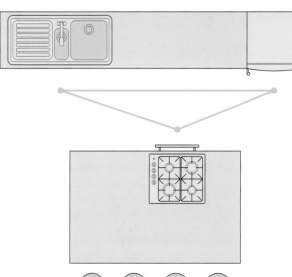

The **ISLAND** kitchen is only suitable for large rooms with a lot of available floor space. An island can be introduced into a large U-shaped or L-shaped kitchen to give a more compact work triangle. Islands create a separate working area and can be used for storage, a hob or a sink, but bear in mind that plumbing and electrical connections will need to run under the floor. Guests can chat to the cook working in the kitchen but will stay out of the way seated on the other side of the island. An island unit can also create a feeling of openness, although careful planning is needed to prevent wasted journeys around it. At its simplest, the island may just be a wooden table around which several people can gather to do the peeling, chopping and slicing.

The **PENINSULA** kitchen is another way of creating a compact kitchen area in a large room (see page 28). The jutting-out worktop can be used as a breakfast bar or to house one of the key activity areas.

BEYOND THE TRIANGLE

Don't feel you must adhere rigidly to the work triangle rule. It is a good basic principle of organisation, but today's kitchens function very differently from those of 50 years ago. The human element is equally if not more important than scientific principles. Only you will be able to identify your cooking habits, your storage requirements and where you like to eat, and if these conflict with the work triangle, you can choose to ignore it. It is better to get the correct layout for your needs than sticking rigidly to a rule.

For instance, if you consider cooking to be an inclusive activity, it may make sense to widen the work triangle and add a second sink and work area so that family and friends can join in. This is also a good way of encouraging children to get involved with cooking from an early age. However if you want to prevent guests helping with the cooking, the kitchen should be laid out so friends are given subtle spatial clues about where they can or cannot linger. The easiest way to do this is to incorporate an island with seating at one end, away from the work area. Parents may also want to situate the hob so that they can keep their eyes on the cooking and on the children in an adjoining room at the same time.

The fridge is the most flexible of the three activity centres in the work triangle. You may choose to move it out of the optimum triangle, since many cooks prefer to take all the ingredients out of cold storage at one time, before they start cooking.

RIGHT: Relaxed and comfortable, the full-length windows in this kitchen instil a sense of eating outdoors and provide a backdrop of natural colour. Seating at the far end of the work surface encourages guests to linger as you cook, but keeps them out of your way.

case study:
THE U-SHAPED KITCHEN

Architect-designed kitchens sound
expensive, but they can offer
surprisingly good value for money,
as well as the opportunity to
reconfigure space. Here the starting
point for architect Steve Turvil was the
creation of a new flat-roofed extension linking the side of the
house and the boundary wall and connecting the kitchen with the
rest of the house. A postwar lean-to which had extended the original kitchen out into the garden
was demolished making a more usable rectangular outdoor space instead of the former L-shape.

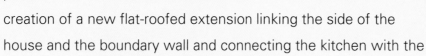

LEFT: One of the client's
stipulations for the new design
was the retention of the Aga.
In the old layout, the Aga had
been located in the corner.
Here it is built in between
cupboards. Instead of blocking
up the window, it was fitted
with sandblasted glass to
provide a natural light source.
RIGHT: Looking across the new
family room/dining area into the
kitchen, which is set down a
step. Flooring in the family
room is solid oak, and in the
kitchen is limestone inset with
small slate squares. The large
wooden chopping board slides
off the slate countertop to
reveal additional gas hobs.

LEFT: The worktop and draining board are made of oak, while cantilevered oak shelves wrap round a pier making a visual connection between kitchen and family room. Some of the shelves are slatted for stacking plates. Because the client wanted to retain a large bullet bin, the shelves are set at a higher level than the worktop to accommodate the bin tucked underneath. **ABOVE:** Custom-designed vegetable drawers in perforated aluminium with oak handles. **RIGHT:** The double-doored fridge is built into the wall. Additional storage space is provided by a generous walk-in larder, built into what was formerly a corridor. Other cupboards are faced with spray-lacquered moisture-resistant MDF.

DESIGN SERVICE

Most high street specialists offer a free design and planning service. However some companies, particularly the top-end, bespoke manufacturers, will view the plan as their own property until you have agreed to buy a kitchen from them. This means that you can only use that kitchen design if you choose that company.

The planning process usually begins with a house visit to measure the room, although most of the large DIY stores will ask you to do this yourself (see Resources, page 213 on how to measure accurately).

Then the retailer should discuss in detail what you want from the kitchen. This should include a whole series of questions to ascertain what you like and dislike about your current kitchen (if there is one), to find out about your style of life and priorities and to set the budget for the work you want done (see Resources, page 211). Of course, as well as the functional element, there will also be a question of aesthetics. What style of kitchen do you prefer? What colours, materials and decoration do you lean towards? What is the decor of the rest of your house? Have you seen or do you have any pictures of kitchens that you admire? It will help and save time if you have as many answers ready as soon as you meet with the kitchen designer, retailer or architect. A specialist is there to suggest options, offer expert advice and answer your queries or concerns, but at the end of the day it is your kitchen, and only you know what will suit you. Similarly, be wary of a specialist who doesn't ask you any or enough relevant questions. This is the groundwork on which your future kitchen will rest, and one instance where more is definitely more.

Once you and your designer have ascertained exactly what you want from your kitchen, and how it should look, the dimensions can be translated into a scaled plan, either as a hand-drawn illustration or as a computerised assimilation. Most kitchen specialists now offer CAD (computer-aided design) planning packages which give you an accurate perspective of how your finished kitchen will look, as a colour photo-realistic 3-D plan on a computer screen. As well as giving you a good idea of how the kitchen will function and look, changes can be made quickly and simply. For example, door fronts can be swapped for a different style, or wall cupboards replaced with open shelving if the room appears too cramped. Virtual reality software is also available, and allows you to 'walk around' your kitchen and view every perspective in simulated daylight and dusk.

When you are happy with the layout, you can take home a printout to consider, before making any final decisions.

Working with an architect

Architects don't just design vast corporate office blocks or expensive loft apartments, they also renovate houses – and parts of houses. Commissioning an architect to design your kitchen is a particularly good idea if you are planning to transform your whole house. This way the kitchen will form part of an overall blueprint that flows with the rest of the structure. An architect can also sort out any planning permissions and building regulations, help find other professionals and get the best price from builders.

Magazine features, architectural organisations and personal recommendation are the best routes to find an architect. Call a few and look at portfolios and previous jobs. Don't be put off by the preconception that architects are expensive. An architect's fee depends on the service the client requires. A full service involves initial meetings to discuss what you want and how the architect perceives the project to work. Then, a brief is drawn up covering design, function, running costs, budget and timing, accompanied by sketches and detailed plans. After obtaining planning permission, they will monitor the subcontractors to make sure the work and materials are up to standard. For this type of service an architect will usually charge a percentage of the final contract sum. The fee will also depend whether the project is a new-build or alteration to an existing building. You could save money by dealing with the building work yourself, but if something goes wrong, an architect will have the objectivity and expertise to deal with it.

A fully equipped island unit with a sink, hob and plenty of worktop space has been planned with precision, creating a one-piece kitchen that blends unobtrusively with this large sunny room. Good design is essential in a big space to avoid wasted journeys around the island.

UNIVERSAL DESIGN

Few kitchens are single-person operations. The people who use your kitchen will all vary: tall and short, old and young, able and less able.

Universal design, also called multi-generational design, bridges the gap. It is a loose blueprint for a kitchen that can be used regardless of age or disability; whether it's deterring a four-year-old from scampering up a chair or enabling an 80-year-old with arthritis to turn on the tap. The basic principle is to amplify ability rather than handicap the less able. With careful layout and sound advice, a universal kitchen will let older people remain in their family home and also allow grandchildren to experiment with cooking. At the same time, the kitchen can be a beautiful and ergonomic space for all generations to use.

ABOVE: A mid-height, side-opening oven suspended from the worktop and moveable base units means that this kitchen is not only stylish, but also flexible and practical for a less mobile user.

RIGHT: A trio of moveable storage units have been custom built to fit the space below the worktop. Each one can be pulled out to create extra worktop space and make cleaning more accessible.

Today, most skilled designers and architects should be able to create a good-looking, universal kitchen without it feeling institutionalised. Look at as many kitchens as you can, talk to friends and advisers, and, if possible, visit a disabled living centre where there will be kitchens on display.

To allow for comfortable wheelchair turning, a space of not less than 1.4m x 1.4m is required where toe recesses are provided under the base fixtures; 1.5m x 1.5m where they are not. It is equally important that there should not be too much space so that the user does not have to manoeuvre the wheelchair excessively – a maximum clear dimension of 1.8m is suggested.

Try out different working heights before making a final decision on work surfaces. Recommended heights are 0.8m for wheelchair users and 0.9m for ambulant disabled people. Remember, for wheelchair users, a knee recess is needed at the sink and food preparation areas – the recommended minimum height is 0.65m with a 0.6m depth.

Opinion favours a U-shaped or L-shaped kitchen with concentrated cooking, storage and washing-up areas. These are also useful for those with difficulty lifting and carrying as it allows items to be pushed along the work surface.

Planning considerations

Remember that people don't come in one size or have similar physical advantages. Consider the following points.

Appliances

▸ Electric appliances are better for those with physical challenges, as they are easier to operate. Electric ovens contain no carbon monoxide or combustibles – someone with impaired smell might not detect a gas leak.

▸ The microwave is the best appliance for the universal kitchen. It doesn't produce combustible gases, cooks quickly and is easy and safe to operate. Plastic containers can be used which are lighter and do not conduct heat. Talking microwaves can assist the elderly and visually impaired.

▸ Front controls mean you don't have to reach over a hot hob while electronic touch controls are easy to operate.

▸ A lift-up hob guard offers protection from the hot elements for children and the visually impaired.

▸ Raising the dishwasher about 250mm off the floor will avoid the need to bend down and reduce back strain.

▸ Siting the oven and microwave also at mid-height level is particularly useful for wheelchair users. Otherwise, a smaller, tabletop version will minimise bending.

▸ Side-opening oven doors allow easier access.

▸ Go for visual contrasts so areas and controls are easier to see, which will help to prevent potential accidents. Opt for black heating elements on a white hob top or white ceramic elements in a metal or black hob.

▸ Controls can be adapted with tactile or Braille markings for people with a visual impairment.

Sinks and taps

▸ Shallow sinks are easier to reach into and provide more clearance underneath.

▸ A rise-and-fall sink centre has been developed which can be raised or lowered at will to suit the user. It is operated electronically or manually, and is perfect for households where height of user varies, or if the kitchen is shared by a chair-bound person and able-bodied family members.

▸ Single lever taps are easier to use for the less dextrous, especially those with a long lever that can be operated with the elbow. Electronically controlled, touch-sensitive taps turn on by waving your hand under the tap and breaking the infrared beam.

Furniture and fittings

▸ A roll-out base unit on wheels can be moved under the worktop or out of the way when necessary.

▸ Shallow shelves ensure easy access.

▸ Tall, pull-out storage units and door-mounted racking allow easy access to stored items.

▸ Pull-out or flap-down kitchen tables will provide extra work space and can retract for wheelchair passage.

▸ Wheelchair users need a space measuring 760 x 1200mm beside the kitchen table for eating comfortably.

ECO-FRIENDLY KITCHENS

Organic food is increasingly popular and widely available, but you should also consider the cooking environment itself. There are plenty of materials and equipment available that will create a hardwearing, stylish kitchen but also present less of a threat to the environment.

Buying reclaimed and antique furniture is a good way of cutting down on wastage. Visit reclamation yards and antique shops and look for pieces that can be incorporated into your kitchen, such as Belfast sinks and reconditioned 1950s fridges. Many furniture makers will adapt old pieces to new forms and uses.

If you are buying a brand-new timber kitchen, look for companies with a responsible attitude to the environment. Choose a company that uses wood grown from sustainable sources and check for certificates of authenticity. Some may also recycle wood shavings, use offcuts as firewood and plant trees in their local community as a goodwill gesture.

Try to select materials which will last and can be easily repaired rather than ones that will have to be replaced. Wood is a good choice for worktops, particularly European hardwoods like oak, beech and maple, which are strong and easy to maintain. Avoid tropical hardwoods such as teak, iroko and wenge, unless they are bought from reclamation or salvage yards.

Flooring too is most environmentally friendly when it is made from durable materials that do not need frequent replacement. An untreated solid wood floor finished with a natural oil or wax is more ecologically sound than laminated flooring which has a high synthetic content. Bamboo is also available as a floor and worktop and being a grass rather than a hardwood, it is extremely fast growing (it can grow up to 1m a day) so plantations are quickly replenished. Stone flooring is also long lasting, although reclaimed stone is preferable to newly quarried stone, and it may have an interesting history to add to its character.

If you experience sensitivity or allergies to conventional paints, try a natural alternative. Instead of using petro-chemicals, environmentally friendly paints use linseed oil

LEFT: Reclaimed wooden worktops are solid, weighty and hardwearing. and add an idiosyncratic charm. The look is complemented by the original wood flooring and hefty butcher's block. Against plain walls, the character of such features stands out. **BELOW:** Using a modern mix of glass and steel frame, this kitchen extension leads onto luxuriant greenery. The contemporary structure not only injects a huge amount of light and airiness into the room, but complements the clean lines of the limestone worktop, pure white cupboards and heavy Butlers sink.

and natural raw materials and can be tinted with mineral and earth pigments such as ultramarine blue and red iron oxide. Conventional paints contain volatile organic compounds (VOCs), mainly solvents, which contribute to air pollution and smog, so look out for paint ranges with a low VOC content. Many natural paints are also virtually odourless and allow you to breathe safely. You can also buy natural, non-toxic wood treatments such as wax, oil, stain and varnish for use on worktops, furniture and floors. And keep an eye out for eco-friendly cleaning products that are biodegradable; avoid petrochemicals, synthetic fragrances, animal testing and chlorine bleaches.

Those with a garden or field would be wise to recycle a mound of general household rubbish using a bonfire and a properly built compost heap. Grassmowings, weeds, vegetable peelings and dead leaves can all be used to make a rich, healthy fertiliser and soil conditioner for the garden, all for free. Compost heaps should be moist but not wet and protected from excessive rain, which will 'leach' the nutrients you are trying to save.

FITTED OR UNFITTED?

Once you have the basic layout of your kitchen in place you need to decide whether you want a fitted or unfitted look. Smart banks of streamlined, fitted units that neatly contain every one of your appliances were once the number one choice for the kitchen-buying public. But a resurgence in 'modular-style' kitchens has created a division between the fitted and unfitted look.

A modular, unfitted design breaks with the traditional idea of planning a kitchen around banks of fitted units. Instead, the basic premise harks back to the fifties when kitchens were put together piece by piece. The modern take offers individual, freestanding elements, each one housing a different kitchen function: cooking modules with a hob and built-in oven; washing-up elements with sink and drainer; and preparation centres with worktop and storage space. The traditional island unit has also been given a facelift to become a sleek, laboratory-style workbench that

is now often the centrepiece of the kitchen, complete with appliances and storage space. This look is very chic and very sophisticated. Most modules use a combination of materials such as aluminium, etched glass and coloured lacquers and stand on chiselled legs to create an airy, open feel.

If you have a smaller kitchen, it is probably best to opt for a fitted kitchen where every last millimetre of space can be utilised with good planning and design. But unfitted kitchens do offer many advantages. They are incredibly flexible and you can build up your own design with different elements and create your own unique, mix-and-match style by adding an old distressed dresser or a bold retro-style fridge-freezer. It allows you to tailor your kitchen to suit your lifestyle and the look of your home.

Unfitted kitchens can also be bought piece by piece, so you don't have to spend a substantial amount of money immediately as you would with a fitted design. You could start with a hob and oven unit while retaining the existing

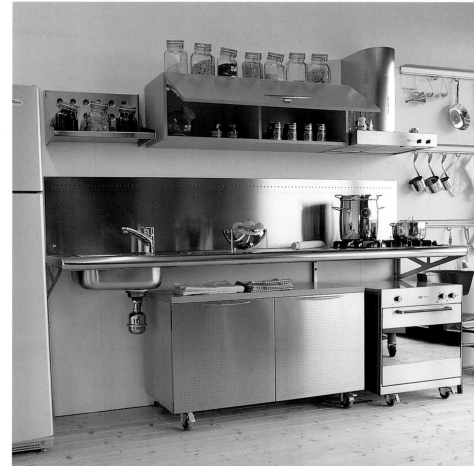

FAR LEFT: A mobile drinks trolley provides extra storage for everyday cooking utensils. **LEFT:** A carefully balanced combination of fixed wall storage and moveable base units breaks up the uniformity of this single-line kitchen. The steel fronts and exposed sink ensure it retains an eclectic, but contemporary flavour.

ABOVE: A reconditioned 1950s oven and a wall-mounted boiler add an idiosyncratic twist to this modern kitchen. The bright, spacious room makes good use of freestanding furniture with natural light flooding in through the full-length windows. **RIGHT:** Translucent glass, shiny metal and pure white walls keep this modular kitchen open and airy.

LEFT: The mix of fitted units and sculptural workbench on legs is the key to this efficient, streamlined work space. The clean lines are echoed by two uninterrupted shelves, stacked with irregular piles of white crockery and glassware and a wall of clear glass windows. **BELOW:** Classic, Shaker-style units are smartly offset by an industrial cookcentre and a useful wood-topped, butcher's block on castors. **BELOW RIGHT:** Flexible kitchen design makes perfect sense in a one-space home such as this. The island unit is made of two mobile units with raised edges along the back and sides, so that the food preparation is not on full view when facing those in the living area. The units can be wheeled closer to the appliances when cooking or moved out of the way when not in use.

built-in units, and add more as funds permit and your plans develop. Perhaps best of all, an unfitted kitchen is also a portable kitchen, so you can simply pack it up and take the whole lot with you when you move house. With this in mind, it is probably worth investing in good-quality units that will stand the test of time.

The choice rests mainly on taste and in reality most kitchens contain both fitted and unfitted elements.

Modular appliances

In the last few years, freestanding kitchen appliances have been transformed into big, beautiful 'focus' machines. From the larger-than-life fridge-freezer, to the cool, aluminium dishwasher and the range cooker in all its guises, these are appliances that make a statement as soon as you walk into the kitchen and can be used to great effect to break up a line of uniform fitted units and add a striking edge to an otherwise ordinary kitchen.

The natural progression of this trend is the introduction of 'modular' appliance units. These stand-alone modules take built-in appliances out of fitted units and house them in tall freestanding frames or columns. Each module can include one or two kitchen functions, say a microwave and fridge, or a single oven and dishwasher. They can be used individually as freestanding elements or be integrated into your existing kitchen.

The look takes its cue from the professional kitchen – units are angular, sleek and usually made from stainless steel. There are also low-level modules with sinks and hobs to complete the deconstructed look. This piece-by-piece approach allows you to build up your kitchen as you like and offers numerous layout possibilities. The key is flexibility, but make sure you take time and seek advice when planning this type of kitchen – modular units do not use space as efficiently as a built-in kitchen.

ABOVE RIGHT: The single line of units is echoed by the rectangular dining table, which is close enough to enable hot food to be served quickly to diners. **BOTTOM LEFT:** The fitted kitchen takes on a whole new meaning with this 'kitchen-in-a-box' design, where appliances and gadgets can be hidden away. **BOTTOM RIGHT:** This kitchen exploits the corner space of this open-plan mezzanine. The combination of steel fronts and pale wood is unobtrusive but modern. **RIGHT:** An island unit is a good way of subtly blurring the boundaries between eating and dining while retaining a feeling of openness. A sweeping apex ceiling with exposed beams is the perfect foil to this neat fitted kitchen.

case study: THE FITTED/UNFITTED KITCHEN

Combining fitted contemporary elements with freestanding traditional pieces, the kitchen in this Manhattan loft provides a hospitable place for cooking and entertaining. When Jan Hashey and Yasuo Minagawa commissioned architect Deborah Berke to come up with a design, the entire space was raw, with concrete ceilings, walls and floors. Her robust approach was to use a palette of simple materials and off-the-peg fittings to complement the clients' collection of salvaged and junk shop finds. Although the rest of the loft has a more minimal quality, maximising the sense of space, the clients wanted the kitchen to be a place where they could display their collection of Japanese pots and crockery and entertain guests while cooking. Directly leading from the kitchen is an open dining area.

FAR LEFT: The centrepiece of the layout is an old marble-topped kitchen table with turned legs, which originally came from the area around the couple's upstate weekend home. Although the table is not valuable, it is very fragile and had to be shipped as an art object to prevent damage in transit. A steel rail provides hanging space for pots and pans over a huge 6-ring steel range; the double-door stainless steel fridge is built in. Flooring is extra-wide wood planking; exposing the feet of the fitted units enhances the feeling of space. **LEFT:** The counter, with its integral splashback, is made of concrete; cabinetry is in maple. The wall-mounted wooden storage unit provides a place to display a superb collection of Japanese pots and crockery.

ESSENTIAL SERVICES

When altering or installing services such as electricity, gas and water, you must employ a professional electrician and plumber. Find one either by personal recommendation (your kitchen company, friends or relatives) or by contacting a professional trade body. These professional bodies should be able to give you a list of reputable members and may offer guarantees and insurance against negligence.

It is crucial that work is coordinated when employing different professionals. For instance, call in a plumber before the subfloor, insulation, plastering and plasterboard are installed. Also, plan as far in advance as possible and decide which appliances you are likely to need in your new kitchen, even those you want at a later date, so that the installation of supply and waste pipes, gas mains and electrical wiring can be achieved in one simple and economical operation.

Plumbing

Your kitchen may only require water pipes to the sink and dishwasher and a gas supply to the oven. However, brief the plumber if you require a waste disposal unit, hot-water dispenser or water-purification system, for example.

Cold-water drinking taps should branch directly off the rising main and not the storage cistern. Different areas of the country have different water. If your water leaves a bad taste in your mouth or is foul smelling, a water-purification system is the best antidote. This has a carbon filter to trap sediment and combat odours. Hard water can cause many problems; mineral salts cause scale build-up on electric heating elements, and inside boilers and radiators. In addition, soap will be difficult to lather and basins will have stubborn scum marks. A whole-house water softener can prevent the damaging effects of hard water by converting these salts into sodium salts, which do no harm. It should be connected into the rising main after the branch to the kitchen cold tap since it is actually healthier to drink hard water than soft.

Drains from sinks and waste disposal units should be fitted with a trap to prevent unpleasant odours coming back into the room and to provide an easily accessible stop valve so any blockages can be cleared from the drainpipe.

Lead pipes carry a serious health hazard. If your house or apartment contains lead pipes, try to negotiate with your plumber. Some will waive installation fees and install replacement pipes for free because the lead ones can be sold as scrap to salvage yards.

Gas

Because of its explosive nature, natural gas should only be installed by a qualified professional. Consult a professionally registered tradesman before you move gas appliances and when you have a new gas oven and hob installed.

Electricity

The electricity supply in your kitchen should always be earthed to prevent appliances from becoming live. Ensure that there are plenty of accessible sockets, that equipment is in good repair and there are no trailing or frayed leads. If you have just moved house, especially into an older building, or are rewiring your kitchen or installing new power points, have the electrical system tested by a registered electrician. Look for a professional body whose duty it is to protect consumers against the hazards of unsafe and unsound electrical installations, as it can supply a list of approved, technically competent contractors, plus a formal, established complaints procedure should the work not be carried out to the council's standards. It is always best to employ a professional electrician to fit and wire sockets as well as high-wattage appliances such as cookers and water heaters.

If you are planning from scratch, think about your lighting scheme – whether or not you want dimmers, two-way switches, track or recessed lighting. The challenge is to locate electrical outlets into your plan before the electrician begins installation and before walls, tiles or splashbacks are in place. You should also have a minimum of four sockets for portable electric appliances such as the kettle and toaster, located near the units where machines are kept and away from running water.

Heating

Even though warmth is generated by cooking, you may need an effective heating system. Wet systems use a boiler to heat water, which is then circulated through pipes into radiators. Modern boilers are becoming smaller and more efficient – some wall-mounted boilers are designed to fit neatly inside a kitchen cupboard and blend in with the units. Combination boilers heat cold water directly from the mains when you turn on the tap, so you don't need a hot-water storage cylinder or cold-water tank in your loft.

Radiators are now available in a wide range of materials, colours, shapes and sizes to suit the style and architecture of your kitchen. There are classic, cast-iron column radiators, industrial, low-level tubes and multifunction wall panels that also house shelves, chrome pegs and wooden storage boxes. Glass panel heaters are sleek, chic and produce an even heat by fusing a transparent electrical element between two sheets of glass. Plinth convector heaters fit discreetly into the base of kitchen units and usually have a 'fan-only' setting for hot, summer days. They free up wall space in a small kitchen. Look out for dual-fuel radiators and convectors that can be powered by electricity, so you can get instant warmth even when the central heating is switched off. There are also electric-only models, which are ideal if access to pipework is difficult.

Underfloor heating is unobtrusive and creates an even temperature. Most run off wet systems, circulating hot water through thermoplastic pipes set in concrete, or an underfloor cavity. If you opt for an electric version, a special heating mat is laid on the floor and covered with a self-levelling compound. When set, the floor can be tiled over as normal. Underfloor heating works under any flooring material even timber, but it can be expensive to install.

If your house is heated by a warm-air system, you can easily run a duct into the kitchen and fit a grille. However, warm-air heating can have the disadvantage of stirring up dust and pollen. Combined cooker/boilers run on gas, oil or solid fuel and not only heat the kitchen, but also provide hot water and central heating for radiators around the house.

WHERE TO BUY?

Buying a kitchen is probably one of the most expensive purchases you're ever likely to make and something you will only have to do perhaps two or three times in your lifetime. It can also be one of the most bewildering experiences if you don't know where to go, what to ask and what to expect. Good research is therefore paramount and will help you find the kitchen that is perfect for you, your family, your house and your budget.

There are three main ways to buy a kitchen and, to a large extent, where you go will depend on how much money you wish to spend. Usually the more expensive the kitchen, the better level of service and better quality furniture and fittings you should receive. However, even if you are buying a flat-pack kitchen from a DIY store, you should still be able to avoid substandard goods, shoddy workmanship and poor service. All kitchen manufacturers have to meet rigorous standards set by the industry and you could also investigate warranties that cover you against defective materials or workmanship.

FAR LEFT: This larger-than-life extractor fan protrudes over the entire length of the island. A brave design move, it adds an unexpected industrial element to what is a modern version of the country kitchen. **LEFT:** The preparation area here is made up of everyday utility ware. Ordinary adjustable glass shelving and a plain white worktop are offset by a map of the world used as wallpaper and a length of tough, yachting rubber pulls across to conceal storage beneath. **ABOVE:** The emphasis in this kitchen is on inexpensive efficiency, practical good looks and hardwearing materials.

DIY

Don't be put off by the do-it-yourself label. These days, large stores offer a huge range of styles and design options that echo those at the top end of the market, from cool, contemporary to the more traditional, country look. Most also offer quality brand-name appliances plus sinks, taps, worktops, lighting and flooring.

A free design service is usually available although you may need to take your own measurements into the store, as site visits aren't always on offer. Don't forget to enquire about computer-aided design so you can see your kitchen as a colour, 3-D plan and then get a printout to take home with you to examine at leisure.

DIY kitchens are likely to be of the flat-pack variety for home assembly, although certain stores do offer the option of a rigid, factory-assembled version. Unless you are a trained kitchen fitter or an accomplished amateur, it is wise to call in the professionals. Most DIY chains have an in-house installation service or can recommend fitters in your area. Don't forget to ask for a written quotation for the installation service before you agree. While the price of the kitchen may seem good value for money, extra charges, such as installation and delivery, can easily double the total cost of a new kitchen. Also check what kind of after-sales service the store offers, including helplines and insurance-backed guarantees.

The high street

If you have a larger budget available, an independent kitchen showroom will offer a large selection of brands including German, Italian and French kitchens. Most showrooms will be able to work within a set budget so don't be put off by pricey-looking window displays. They should also offer the same level of service to each customer regardless of how much the kitchen costs.

The high street specialist should be able to take care of the whole job for you – from ripping out your old kitchen to installing lighting, flooring, appliances and cabinets. Ask questions and establish what the service includes, for example, home visits and planning. Nearly all showrooms require a deposit of some kind, but the amount they charge can vary dramatically. As a guideline, expect to pay around 25 per cent of the total cost.

The bespoke kitchen

This is the haute couture of the kitchen world, a design tailormade to suit your ideas, needs and space. A bespoke designer will begin by showing you examples of his designs, then discuss colours, materials and finishes to create a one-off kitchen. This will inevitably require a lot of input from you at the design stage, so make sure you have a fairly firm, but not inflexible idea of what you want from your kitchen before you make any appointments.

To a certain degree, every bespoke manufacturer will specialise in a certain style of kitchen, so avoid the company that is known for its rustic, country look if you want a sleek, modern design. As with any one-to-one service, expect to pay a premium for a bespoke kitchen, so advise them of your budget before you begin work. However, that's not to say this type of kitchen is completely out of your price bracket even if you are working within a restricted budget. Once the designer has presented you with a plan, you could ask about replacing some of the more expensive materials with cheaper alternatives to keep costs down. For example, substituting solid wood cabinets with a wood veneer or granite worktops with a good-quality laminate.

As bespoke companies offer such a personal, one-to-one service, you are likely to form a very good working relationship with your designer, and the after-sales service is usually second to none.

Questions to ask

What does the price include? Make sure you get a detailed quotation that covers every aspect of the job, including fitting, tiling, flooring and any structural alterations you have discussed. Only when you have got an overall price for everything you have asked for, will you be able to make a fair comparison with other quotes.

Is there a free design service? Most showrooms offer this as a free service but check to see that an extra charge isn't added on to your total bill. Some bespoke designers will charge you for plans because they are extremely detailed and can include hand-drawn and computer-designed images.

How long will the job take? Ask how long the kitchen will take to arrive and how long the fitting will take – get a written estimate for extra reassurance. Be prepared to wait some weeks especially if the kitchen has to be ordered from abroad, if it is an unusual size or specification or if you are having made-to-order features.

How strong is the kitchen? Ask what the doors are made of and how sturdy the furniture is. Unless you go for a bespoke kitchen, the carcases will usually be made from melamine-covered chipboard or MDF. These will vary in thickness depending on quality – from 25mm at the budget end of the market up to 30mm for a mid-range kitchen. Bespoke kitchens may have MDF (medium density fibreboard) carcases faced with a matching veneer. Check drawers and hinges and, if possible, choose metal as opposed to plastic. Ensure that the bases are firm – a piece of chipboard stapled to the frame won't last, and if units are in MDF, check that it is water-resistant, chipboard isn't.

Installation

Once you have decided on the final layout of your new kitchen, it is time to call in the professionals, unless you are an expert fitter yourself. Get at least three written quotes from builders, kitchen fitters, plumbers and electricians so that you can compare their prices. As with most matters, recommendation is a good start. If a friend, relative or colleague has had a kitchen installed recently, ask which fitters they used and what they thought of them. The company you are buying your kitchen from may also have their own team of in-house fitters or else a recommended list of skilled and trustworthy tradesmen who will work to high standards.

There are four basic phases to installing a new kitchen: structure, services, finishes and fittings, and then there is the equipment. After you have settled on a kitchen plan, the first thing that must be done is structural work. If there is damp, it must be treated. Then wiring, plumbing and gas installation must be completed. When the shell (the room itself) is finished, the fittings, equipment and appliances can be introduced. The key is to plan in a logical order. For instance, electrical wiring for lights and wall sockets should be done before plastering and tiling; appliances ideally should be installed after flooring is laid.

If building work is going on at the same time, the new kitchen should be delivered only when construction is complete and the room is ready. Most companies need to be satisfied that the kitchen will not be damaged by prevailing site conditions, such as new plaster, or used by other tradespeople working at the premises. To promote good teamwork, introduce the different tradesmen to each other and make sure they understand each other's requirements. Ask for a schedule of work from everyone involved so you can monitor each stage as it progresses. If building work runs over and your kitchen cannot be delivered on the agreed fit date, check that it can be stored for no extra cost.

There are three different types of 'fit'. A 'dry fit' includes installing furniture and appliances, but not making the final connections of the appliances. Any waste generated by the kitchen installation is removed but the price does not include stripping out existing furniture. A 'wet fit' is the same as dry fit but also includes all plumbing and electrical connections, while a 'turn-key' operation is a combination of dry and wet fits plus all finishes including paintwork and flooring; in other words, the complete job.

After the job is finished, allocate a drawer or dedicated space to keep all the information about the maintenance of your kitchen units, worktops, tiles and flooring. Start a file and include maintenance manuals for your equipment and appliances, guarantees and servicing documents. A tool kit can also prove indispensable in the kitchen.

Once you have considered the basics of planning, determined the best layout for your kitchen and, crucially, decided where it should be located with respect to other areas in the home, you can begin to think about the kitchen as a space or room in its own right. As with any other area in the home, this partly entails exploring issues to do with colour, pattern and texture, basic elements that comprise the decorative palette. But in this context it is equally important to pay attention to those individual or idiosyncratic touches that express a sense of character and personality. The preferences you express elsewhere in your home shouldn't stop short at the kitchen door.

Kitchen Living

The idea of the kitchen as a space worthy of decorative consideration would have vastly entertained our great-grandparents, for whom the kitchen was the largely unseen engine room behind the green baize door. As long as kitchens remained the domain of servants, there was no question of fitting, furnishing or decorating them with anything in mind beyond practical utility. Of course, many such kitchens, particularly those extensive service areas 'below stairs' found in the great country houses, have their own elemental appeal; I have always particularly admired the scrubbed simplicity of traditional larders, still rooms, pantries and dairies. But in most ordinary households, the kitchen was generally a fairly inhospitable place, badly lit, poorly ventilated and soberly decorated to disguise the discoloration caused by coal-fired stoves and gas lighting.

After the successive social upheavals following two world wars, when the average kitchen had become a one-person, or more accurately, one-woman operation, huge emphasis was placed on efficiency and ergonomics. Inspired by fitted kitchen designs originally developed in the United States in the 1920s, and equipped with the latest labour-saving appliances, many postwar kitchens resembled nothing so much as miniature domestic production lines, clad in new easy-clean laminates, floored in the ubiquitous linoleum or vinyl and lit with flickering fluorescent tubes.

Reaction to the sterility of these environments, and a growing informality of lifestyle from the 1960s onwards, saw the kitchen dressed up in any number of styles: townhouses had their 'country' kitchens; the latest modern appliances were concealed behind Edwardian-style decor panels; acres of stainless steel elevated the home cook to the food technician.

Today, kitchens no longer have a point to prove. The fully fitted bespoke kitchen is still a status symbol and there are plenty of people who are prepared to invest huge sums of money to make that kind of statement. But a more relaxed

LEFT: A glazed ceiling bathes a kitchen area in natural light, providing optimum conditions for cooking. An indoor swing reflects the easy informality of this airy open-plan space.
RIGHT: Coloured fairy lights add a quirky personal touch to a kitchen-diner, simply furnished with freestanding appliances and fittings, including an old butcher's block.

approach is becoming increasingly popular, where old and new, fitted and unfitted elements work happily together. This is not to say that kitchen 'style' is now an irrelevance, rather that people are beginning to accept that it can emerge partly through personal taste, partly as a response to context and, crucially, as an expression of the way they want to live.

Accordingly, instead of presenting a range of kitchen 'styles' this chapter is organised according to different patterns of kitchen use. The sections are not intended to be watertight, merely to distil some common themes that inform design and decoration. Although the type of kitchen that would suit a busy professional is unlikely to be adequate for a family with young children, distinctions are not always so clear cut and you may well find yourself picking different elements to suit your own surroundings and needs.

An obvious parameter for most people is the amount of space they have at their disposal. But as the previous chapter on planning has demonstrated, a small kitchen does

not mean that you should restrain your ideas; spatial limitations can often be overcome by clever planning, both of the notional kitchen space and the home as a whole.

Space is a critical issue, but it can be just as important to spend some time thinking about how you like to cook and by extension how you like to live. You don't necessarily have to have a hungry family to cater for to benefit from an inclusive kitchen, for example – this pattern would also suit single people who like to entertain. Those wedded to traditional methods of cooking or those with a taste for robust simplicity might equally appreciate the elemental qualities of a vernacular kitchen. While keen gardeners are obvious candidates for kitchens that merge with outdoor spaces, many people relish any opportunity to move outside, weather permitting.

Successful kitchens are founded on careful planning; kitchens where you want to spend time are those that reflect how you live.

LEFT: Intense shades are increasingly seen in the kitchen. Deep orange walls create a lively and hospitable background. 'White goods', the old term for household appliances, are now available in a range of strong accent colours. **ABOVE:** Here, colour accentuates spatial planning, adding a welcome level of interest to a sleek fitted area.

LEFT AND BELOW: A space-age update of the old serving hatch, this extra-deep opening, within a fitted storage wall, provides a visual link between kitchen and eating area, allowing natural light to penetrate the kitchen. The glossy finish on the units was achieved with five coats of polyurethane lacquer.

BELOW RIGHT: A simple run of white base units with a stainless steel splashback is lifted out of the ordinary by a playful approach to decoration. Kitchens are now increasingly emerging as living areas in their own right, a trend that has been signalled by a heightened interest in colours and finishes.

Decorative choices

Even the most cursory glance through a pile of brochures from manufacturers, suppliers and retailers is enough to indicate the huge breadth of choice facing consumers today. Where safe neutral shades, uniformly white appliances and smooth synthetic textures once used to predominate, there has been something of a decorative explosion.

This breadth of choice is particularly evident when it comes to colour. White, with its connotations of purity, hygiene and freshness, has always had a strong association

with kitchens. Perhaps it all goes back to that familiar combination of white and blue which was such a feature of traditional dairies and still rooms (blue was believed to act as a fly-repellent). With the emergence of the fitted kitchen in the early decades of the twentieth century, white was widely adopted as a hallmark of domestic efficiency and good housekeeping; it's not surprising that household appliances are popularly termed 'white goods'.

Similarly, the country kitchen aesthetic accounts for the long-standing popularity of neutral decorative schemes. Buffs, creams, browns, terracottas and off-whites are the natural partners of kitchen schemes featuring surfaces made of wood, brick, stone and tile.

In recent years, however, the kitchen has shrugged off its neutral image and embraced strong colour, a change that signals the transformation of the kitchen from behind-the-scenes workroom to living area in its own right. Where kitchen colour was once restricted to those incidental accents provided by enamelled saucepans, for example, or a platter of fresh fruit or vegetables, it is increasingly employed in a more positive and deliberate fashion to define space, enhance light and generate mood and atmosphere. White goods themselves are white no longer, but available in every conceivable shade from navy blue to shocking pink, as much a part of the design scheme as a working appliance.

In the kitchen, as in any interior, colour can be used to enhance the effect of natural light. Light, airy backgrounds make a space seem brighter and more spacious; warmer,

FAR LEFT TOP: 'Bookworm', Ron Arad's innovative approach to shelving complements the sleek curve of the kitchen counter. **FAR LEFT BOTTOM:** A glossy blue rubber floor demarcates a kitchen area, a material shift that is as much about practicality as aesthetics. The neat coverstrip between the kitchen flooring and the natural fibre carpet in the main living area is a key detail here. **LEFT:** Colour can be immensely uplifting; even small touches of colour create a positive effect. A single wall picked out in a warm red serves as a vivid backdrop for the display of children's artwork.

richer tones provide a cosy sense of enclosure. At the same time, vibrant planes of colour, picking out a single wall or horizontal surface, can serve to delineate space, which can be particularly valuable in an open-plan, multi-purpose area. A robust and confident use of colour also helps to generate a sense of vitality, even personality, signalling the kitchen's wider role as living area.

In many ways, texture is just as important as colour and in some instances can even stand in for it. In its proper sense (that is, when it is not merely a question of setting the microwave), cooking is an activity which relies heavily on touch and feel: the 'hands-on' nature of kitchen work only goes to heighten our awareness of texture in the surfaces with which we regularly come into contact. For this reason, seamless kitchens where surfaces are uniformly smooth can be rather uneasy, characterless places and serve to undermine our enjoyment and appreciation of food with all our senses.

The more subdued the colours, the greater the emphasis on texture should be to provide a sense of character and depth. Highly reflective surfaces, such as stainless steel, glass and glazed ceramic tiles, add a sparkling crispness to a decorative scheme. Matt surfaces such as wood and certain types of stone provide a subtle tactility. In many cases, textural variety is a natural outcome of material choice. A scheme that features different materials used as flooring, work surfaces or on the walls will often have in-built textural character.

Synthetics have their place in kitchen design and new types of plastic, particularly lighter and more translucent forms of polypropylene, are vast improvements on dreary postwar artificial materials. But in the context of texture, natural materials will always have the edge, simply because they age so well and have the potential to improve with wear and sympathetic maintenance. Battered plastic or scratched laminate utterly lacks the charm of a wooden surface that has been subjected to the same treatment.

Where there is textural character, inevitably there is also pattern: the flecked surface of granite, the grain of wood, the gridded appearance of tile and mosaic are all patterns of a sort. What is infinitely less successful, and worse,

RIGHT: The quality of light, both natural and artificial, adds vitality to neutral surroundings. In this all-white kitchen, light from a skylight is supplemented by spotlights over the worktop and a large photographer's spot that illuminates the living area. **INSET RIGHT:** Material quality speaks for itself. A pale marble worktop complements the stone tiled flooring, which extends to the outdoor area. **FAR RIGHT:** Pale and interesting: a luminous effect has been achieved by painting a wooden floor white and tiling kitchen surfaces in grey mosaic. The dining table is a white painted MDF top over a steel base.

ABOVE A subtle combination of materials, from painted to natural wood, stainless steel to mosaic, provides inherent depth of character that complements the mixture of traditional elements, such as the Belfast sink, and more contemporary detailing. **BELOW:** A portion of wall painted with blackboard paint provides a handy space for messages and reminders, and a good alternative to a noticeboard. **RIGHT:** A stainless steel work surface and appliances are set off by Op-art-inspired patterns that have been laminated onto a dining table and unit fronts. Wall and base units are uniform to emphasise the graphic nature of the scheme.

utterly depressing is where pattern is used to 'prettify' or somehow distract one's attention away from the essentially utilitarian or practical nature of the kitchen. Decorative motifs on kettles and toasters, stencilled drawer fronts, even patterned paper kitchen towel are all examples of this meretricious use of pattern to embellish what ought to be allowed to speak for itself. Rather more sympathetic in the kitchen context, however, are retro patterns from the 1950s or 1960s, which can add a quirky, tongue-in-cheek quality...if used sparingly!

Pattern adds vitality, movement and rhythm to the interior. In this sense, it is less about superfluous decorative flourish and more about arrangement. A row of spice jars, bottles of oils, vinegars and wines, beautiful graphics on food packaging, a random collection of fridge magnets, an appetising display of fresh fruit and vegetables, or a sculptural array of cooking utensils are all natural kitchen patterns that delight the eye.

case study: KITCHEN COLOUR

Colour is uniquely uplifting, but it is also a good way of delineating space. In this open-plan living/working/eating space in London, a singing shade of bright yellow defines a kitchen area. The single-level house was designed in 1968 by the celebrated architect Richard Rogers, for his mother. Today, it is the home of Rogers' son, Ab, his partner Sophie Braimbridge and their daughter, Ella. Both Ab, who is a furniture designer, and Sophie, a chef and food writer, work from home and the inclusivity of the space is a positive bonus. A unifying feature is the glossy epoxy resin flooring, which, like the bold colour scheme, has remained unchanged since the house was first designed.

LEFT: The bright yellow island runs almost the whole length of the space. On the 'living' side it is fully fitted with capacious storage cupboards. **ABOVE:** On the 'kitchen' side, the island houses all the working elements, with the preparation area concealed behind an upstand. Taps are mounted directly onto the upstand to make full use of the available space, with servicing routed through the internal structure of the island. Along with a wood-fired pizza oven in the garden, the kitchen provides the perfect place for Sophie to test recipes and plan cookery courses. Ab's computer workstation is set up to one side of the dining area.

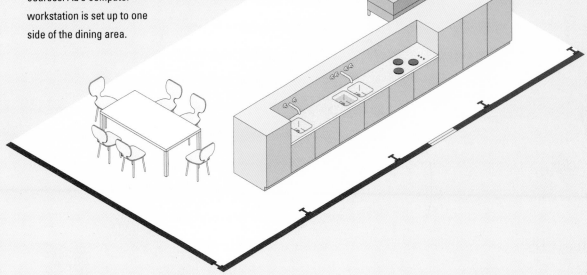

THE INCLUSIVE KITCHEN

Embracing a wide range of household activities, many of which may have little to do with either cooking or eating, the inclusive kitchen is a flexible pattern that has become increasingly popular in recent years. This particular category includes kitchen-diners, multi-purpose cooking/eating/living areas and large family kitchens that act as a nerve centre for the entire household.

Like many trends in interior design, the inclusive kitchen is not so much a new idea as an old idea newly discovered. Centuries before houses were subdivided into rooms, each with its own assigned function, the hall house of the Middle Ages was basically a single enclosed space with a central hearth, around which all the activities of the household took place, the most critical being cooking and eating.

Of course, the inclusive kitchen does not represent an attempt to turn back the clock to a medieval lifestyle, or even a conscious reinvention of this ancient pattern. But it does imply a similar lack of hierarchy in the way domestic life is organised and an absence of the distinction between what goes on behind the scenes and what is open to view.

The central feature of the inclusive kitchen is a certain generosity of spirit. It's a place where everyone can muck in together to prepare a meal, sit down to eat it and clear up afterwards. It's where children can absorb some of the basic skills involved in cooking through sheer proximity to the main focus of activity; where parents can keep an eye on youngsters playing or doing their homework. It's somewhere friends and visitors can drop by and instantly feel welcome; inevitably, in households where there are pets, it's also where you'll find the dog basket or the cat curled up in a patch of sun.

If it is generous in spirit, the inclusive kitchen need not necessarily occupy vast amounts of floor area. Paradoxically, this particular pattern often works just as well where space is limited as it does when there is plenty of room to play around with. If you're short of space, the kitchen per se can be no more than a compact functional zone slotted into a general living area. One of the advantages of this arrangement is that it combines a feeling of spaciousness with the ease of operation that results when kitchens are tightly planned.

LEFT: Generous in spirit and size, true industrial-scale lofts provide the perfect setting for the inclusive kitchen. Here the cooking area occupies a corner of the space, with a run of base units serving as a divider.

ABOVE: Another counter-cum-divider demarcates space in an open living/eating/cooking area. With all the fittings and fixtures concealed, the kitchen virtually disappears from view when not in use.

Defining areas

Inclusive kitchens have few physical barriers to separate them from other areas in the home. Decoratively speaking, it is therefore important for the space to read as a coherent whole. One way of achieving this is to use the same colours or materials throughout, so that the planes of walls, ceiling and floor provide a unified backdrop.

At the same time, a multi-purpose space often benefits from a decorative strategy that draws out some distinction between different areas. Accents of strong colour can be used to define areas within the space or suggest a boundary between one area and another: for example, picking out a wall next to a dining table in a vivid shade provides a focus for eating; while a bright kitchen counter can serve as a visual marker between the relaxing or living side of the space and the practical, working side.

More subtle signals can be sent out in the form of changes in materials. It often makes sense to vary materials in an open-plan area, particularly those used for flooring, to address different practical requirements. Where a kitchen area might require the easy maintenance of tiles, linoleum,

resin or similar surfaces, you may wish to provide more comfort underfoot in the space set aside for eating or relaxation. Varying the material but sticking to the same overall colour or tone is the most understated approach, but a decorative shift of gear can be very effective, too, especially in a larger space.

The shape of the room and any existing architectural features can also be useful for adding a sense of definition. L-shaped layouts offer a natural break between activities; alcoves, recesses and redundant chimney breasts can be exploited to create fitted areas for kitchen storage. Any change in level, however minor – a step up or down – can also be used to demarcate different areas; otherwise, you could always manufacture a change in level by constructing a platform to raise the kitchen area up slightly.

The inclusive kitchen means that, for at least some of the time, cooking is going to be an activity carried out in public view. Therefore a degree of separation, no matter how minimal, between functional areas and relaxing or eating areas, is important from both a practical and psychological point of view. If you're a nervous or tentative

FAR LEFT: An open stairway, with sleek metal banister supported on fine steel cabling, separates the cooking and eating end of the room from the main living area. Good-looking modular storage organises clutter in a working wall.

LEFT: Double-height spaces offer alternative ways of defining areas. A room within a room, this kitchen is partly concealed behind a high counter that serves to screen work in progress without isolating the cook.

cook, it helps if every faltering attempt to follow a recipe isn't open to scrutiny. But even if you're a confident show-off, some kind of barrier between the cooking area and the rest of the space can be a useful aid to concentration. Cooking often means working in extreme conditions, in close proximity to searing heat, steam, sharp knives and heavy pans. Whatever helps you to focus on the task in hand is a positive asset.

At the same time, unless you are an exceptionally tidy cook, or scrupulously wash each dirty dish as you go along, kitchen clutter and the detritus that inevitably results from the production of a meal is going to be a bit of an eyesore for those sitting down to enjoy that meal or relaxing afterwards. There will be times, in a multi-purpose space, when you want to forget that the kitchen is there.

A counter with a raised upstand serving to conceal both kitchen debris and the cook's every move is one solution to this problem. An alternative is to locate the kitchen area along the length of a wall, with sliding doors or folding screens that close off the space when it is not in use. Open shelf units also make good spatial dividers without screening off the kitchen area entirely, and are ideal for displaying kitchenalia. Translucent panels running floor to ceiling can screen kitchen clutter without blocking light; if they are folding or sliding you can keep your options open.

Practicalities

The inclusive kitchen can present something of a practical challenge. It's all very well to plan your multi-purpose space so that it functions as one smooth flow of activity from area to area, where meals are prepared and whisked immediately

LEFT: A strategic use of colour highlights different areas of activity within an open space. A robust, freestanding partition partially encloses the kitchen area and screens the hobs. Seamless detailing and well-judged proportions contribute to the success of the result.
BELOW FAR LEFT: Simple but effective apportioning of space creates separate zones for cooking, eating and sleeping within a single area.
BELOW LEFT: A cosier take on the inclusive kitchen features copper-bottomed pans over a traditional range, a dining table fashioned from rough planking and tailored kitchen storage.

Another key practicality is lighting. In the inclusive kitchen, flexibility is essential. Preparation areas, worktops, sinks and hobs need good task lighting so that chopping, cutting and handling sizzling or simmering pans can be carried out safely. Because the level of lighting required for these practical chores is generally higher and more directional in its effect than the type of lighting which is preferable for the sociable activities of eating and relaxing, it is a good idea to have the kitchen lights on a dimmer switch, so you can lower the light levels in the kitchen area when it's time to put food on the table.

An inclusive kitchen, where everyone is welcome, needs some extra consideration when it comes to safety. If very young children or babies are going to be playing in the kitchen – and messing about on the floor with pots and pans and bits of dried pasta has to be one of the top games of toddlerhood – make sure they are not unnecessarily exposed to hazards. Keep flexes well out of reach, turn pan handles away from the edge of the cooker, store powerful and toxic cleansers and household chemicals in a lockable cupboard and install ovens at eye level rather than under counters to prevent accidental burns on hot doors. It's not a bad idea to keep a properly stocked first-aid box on hand in the kitchen, either.

When children play in the kitchen or when they get old enough to tackle their homework on the kitchen table, it makes sense to allocate some storage space for these activities within the kitchen. A cupboard, a lidded box or storage space under banquettes or window seats can provide stowing space for toys, creative materials and games; while dictionaries and reference books can be shelved along with the cookbooks.

Inclusive kitchens inevitably serve as household nerve centres. Keep a step ahead of the game by providing a place where all those vital details – everything from the phone number of the emergency plumber to the rehearsal dates for the school play – can be readily located, such as an old-fashioned bulletin board, a portion of wall painted with blackboard paint or an in-tray by the phone.

to the table. But if that meal is then accompanied by the chugging of the washing machine, or if a thick fug of cooking fumes lingers long into the evening, you haven't thought everything through properly.

All kitchens require good systems of extraction, but in the case of the inclusive kitchen this requirement is particularly acute. Cooking can be a hot, humid activity, generating steam and greasy vapours. While the aroma of food cooking may well be appetising just before you sit down to eat, stale cooking odours can be very off-putting the rest of the time. Invest in a decent ventilation hood and try to arrange the kitchen area so that it benefits from cross-ventilation from opening windows or doors.

It can also be a good idea to exclude some of the noisier appliances from the kitchen itself. Washing machines and tumble dryers are often a feature of kitchen layouts, but they can equally and just as conveniently be installed in an adjacent utility room or even in a bathroom, creating a more peaceful atmosphere.

FAR LEFT: Where there is sufficient ceiling height, raising a kitchen area up a step or two is an effective means of signalling a change of activity. In this serene, light-filled space the kitchen is set on a platform accessed by two shallow steps.

LEFT: A change in level has also been employed in this loft conversion to segregate the cooking and eating area from the general living space. It is important to make the change in level significant enough to avoid the risk of tripping.

THE SMALL KITCHEN

If most people's idea of a dream kitchen tends to be somewhere that is large and open, you might well assume that a small kitchen isn't something you would choose, but something you get forced into by circumstances. Certainly, small kitchens are often synonymous with a general shortage of space all round – first-time homeowners, for example, often find themselves having to compromise in this department. But not everyone wants or needs a capacious kitchen. If you are at that stage in life where you eat out regularly, or if you simply don't enjoy cooking very much, it makes far better sense to allocate less space to the kitchen and keep everything as simple and straightforward as you can.

Some people, however, serious cooks among them, actively prefer small kitchens, arguing that they make better and more efficient work spaces. There is an element of truth in this. If you have ever spent time in a professional kitchen, you will have noticed that chefs hardly ever move from the spot. Whatever they need is right to hand, or there is someone to hand it to them. When a restaurant kitchen is in full swing and the tables are packed with hungry customers, chefs need to be able to concentrate their efforts at the stove and waste as little time and energy as possible trotting to and fro. A small, well-organised kitchen can offer the same degree of control.

These observations are backed up by ergonomic studies of kitchen activity, first carried out in the early 1950s. Such research suggests that the optimum distance between the three points of the 'work triangle' – sink, cooker and fridge

LEFT: In small kitchens, tight planning and careful design are essential to accommodate fittings and fixtures. Here wall-hung lockers store the bulk of kitchen paraphernalia, while a hanging rack keeps frequently used items readily to hand.

ABOVE RIGHT: A complete kitchen is concealed within a custom-designed cabinet with folding doors. **BELOW RIGHT:** Restricting the layout to one wall frees up enough space for a small table, which can double up as an additional worktop.

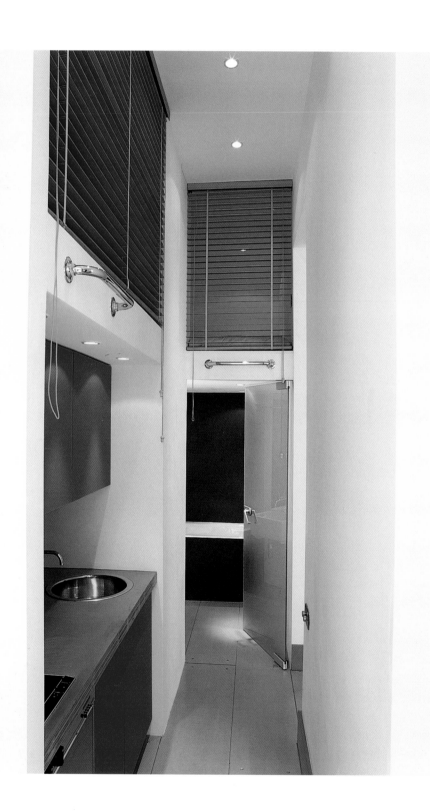

LEFT: Kitchens don't come much more compact than this narrow fitted space. Steel brackets provide anchorage for a ladder to access overhead storage, concealed behind slatted cedar blinds. The floor is MDF, sealed and lacquered; the worktop is stainless steel. A glass door allows light in.

FAR RIGHT: A judicious contrast of materials – warm wood and gleaming stainless steel – provides depth of interest in a compact fitted kitchen.

BELOW: Views through to other areas, but particularly external views, prevent small kitchens from feeling too enclosed.

– should be no more than a few paces at most. Small kitchens may rule out certain things, but ease of operation is not one of them.

What small kitchens do rule out is extraneous clutter. Every piece of equipment, every single fitting and fixture must earn its keep. Enthusiastic cooks often tend to be kitchenware enthusiasts as well, the sort of people who find it difficult to resist the opportunity to acquire yet another utensil or shiny new gadget. But if you have a small kitchen it's also important to bear in mind that many good cooks accomplish much with the bare minimum and many even swear by the back-to-basics approach. A couple of good saucepans, a frying pan, casserole, maybe a wok, a few sharp knives and some basic kit, such as sieves, grater, colander and mixing bowls, are really all you need to cook the most elaborate meals. Kitchen equipment can be very seductive, but before you give that fish-kettle house room think hard about how often you're really going to use it.

If you have to store cutlery and crockery in the kitchen, you need to keep things simple here, too: oven-to-tableware that avoids the need for separate serving dishes; tumblers that you can use for juice, water or wine; mugs instead of cups and saucers; one set of plain plates that you can use both everyday and for special occasions. You'll need less, and what you have will be more uniform in terms of shape and size, which in turn will make it easier to store.

A small kitchen, necessarily, is going to be a single-person operation – there won't be the elbow room for two cooks. It's also going to be a space which is chiefly devoted to cooking. This means you have to be equally ruthless about excluding anything that does not relate directly to this central function. But although a small kitchen is never going to be a living area in the fullest sense, it can be a supremely effective work space and one that is a pleasure to use.

Saving and enhancing space

Successful small kitchens never feel small; compact, certainly, but not confined. To a large extent, this comes down to tight, rigorous planning which exploits every last

millimetre of available space. But it also entails adopting various decorative and design strategies to create the illusion of spaciousness.

The most effective small kitchens are generally fitted, for two reasons. A fitted layout allows you to maximise floor area and avoid unnecessary obstacles and protrusions you have to navigate round, but it also has a neater, more seamless appearance, which is equally as important. A simple, streamlined approach, with appliances slotted in under a clear line of work surface, and walls devoted to hanging racks of utensils and shelving, provides an in-built sense of clarity and order. It is worth spending considerable time at the planning stage to ensure you achieve the optimum layout, not merely to make the best use of the available space, but also to ensure there is nothing awkward about the arrangement. When you don't have much room to spare in the first place, anything which niggles or isn't quite right is bound to become a major source of irritation pretty quickly.

You can also pack more into a small kitchen if you opt for slimline or smaller-scale appliances, but you have to be sure that these will adequately serve your needs and also represent a sensible long-term investment (you may move somewhere larger before the appliances have come to the end of their life). Many kitchen manufacturers offer a range of features that allow you to maximise the storage potential of fitted units: pull-out wire baskets so you can use the full height and depth of cupboards, for example, or Magic Corner units that fit into corners and utilise otherwise dead space. Perhaps most useful are pull-out or flap-down preparation areas. Small kitchens tend to be short of worktop space and such features can make the room much more workable on a daily basis.

Decoratively speaking, simplicity is the key: a limited palette of colours and textures avoids visual busyness which can make the room feel even less spacious that it actually is. Light colours and reflective surfaces such as glass and stainless steel, on the other hand, enhance the sense of

space. Omitting the plinth at the base of fitted units, so that the feet are exposed and the floor is uninterrupted, can also add a sense of visual lightness – just make sure you can clean easily underneath!

Good lighting is essential; recessed or fitted types of lighting, such as downlights, make sense in a small, tightly planned space. You might also consider installing internal windows or portholes in partition walls to provide glimpses through to adjacent spaces and borrow additional natural light. If your small kitchen is also a self-contained room, it might be worth omitting the door altogether and removing the portion of wall above the door head so the entrance to the kitchen runs straight from floor to ceiling. It's a relatively minor change, but it can have the effect of making the kitchen seem much less enclosed.

Small kitchens often succeed or fail on the level of detail. Good-looking handles, neat trim and edges, and well-considered junctions between different surfaces can make all the difference.

BELOW LEFT: When space is tight, simplicity of design and fitting is a good strategy, maximising efficiency and minimising visual clutter.
BELOW RIGHT: A pull-out table top neatly integrated into a storage wall creates space for eating or working. Pull-out or flap-down features are particularly useful in small kitchen design. **RIGHT:** Pivoting opaque glass doors enclose a small kitchen area within an open-plan space, creating a central box or service core, tucked away from the eating area.

case study: THE SMALL KITCHEN

Small spaces leave next to no tolerance for error. Nicole Morgan's tiny London apartment was originally a studio flat, with galleried spaces; the redesign, by architect Misha Stefan, arranged the flat over two levels, three including the roof terrace on top. On the ground-floor level is a bedroom and bathroom, while the living/eating/cooking area is on the first floor where the light is better. Exceptionally tight planning and ingenious spatial strategies now make the whole apartment feel much bigger than it actually is. During the design process, the architect made a cardboard prototype of the basic shapes and tried out a series of different kitchen layouts on Nicole until the fit was absolutely right.

ABOVE RIGHT: Looking from the kitchen through to the adjacent living/dining area. The design challenge was how to fit a practical and workable kitchen within a very narrow 2.5m width. To borrow additional space, the wedge-shaped sink unit is cleverly angled over the stairs. The purple dining table is a classic fold-down design, with the panel fixed on a long piano hinge and supported by a round peg leg. The mosaic tiling around the sink softens the impact of the gleaming stainless steel surfaces.

BELOW RIGHT: The flooring throughout the flat is light maple, which enhances the sense of space. Walls are white universal plaster sealed with varnish. **FAR RIGHT:** At the far end of the kitchen, a plain plasterboard wall neatly encloses the fridge; behind are the steps up to the roof terrace. The cavity under the stairs has been transformed into a handy broom cupboard on the left, and also houses the boiler on the right, separated from the fridge by an insulated partition.

KITCHEN VERNACULAR

The kitchen's association with food and comfort – indeed with nurturing in general – means that for many people vernacular styles of decoration and design continue to exert a strong appeal. Perhaps the best example of this approach is the ever-popular 'country' kitchen, with its scrubbed wooden table, solid fittings, bunches of drying herbs and dresser crammed with crockery and home-made preserves. But country kitchens from any country – the kind one might encounter in a simple holiday villa or beach house – share many similar elements and offer many of the same attractions as the more traditional one.

A key characteristic is simplicity. When so much of modern life is dominated by complex technology, technology that most of us don't understand, can't fully operate and could never begin to fix in the event of breakdown, kitchen vernacular provides a way of regaining control and getting back to a more basic, hands-on way of doing things: Agas rather than microwaves; larders rather than internet-linked fridges; sharp knives rather than food processors and so on.

Another element is continuity. Kitchen vernacular is timeless: neither cutting edge, nor rooted in the past. It is an approach which accommodates both old and new, evoking memories of kitchens we might have known as children, while at the same time promising to outlive the latest trends and fads: the type of kitchen you might add to, or subtract from, but never feel the need to redo.

Contemporary country

It's fair to say that the type of country kitchen you see advertised in brochures bears little resemblance to any true country kitchen, past or present. Heavy on the wood, and even heavier on the reproduction detail, such ranges have long promoted a romantic vision of rural life for the benefit of town-dwellers who live miles from the nearest cow. When 'country' is so often used as a shorthand for 'natural', it's not surprising that people leading stressful urban lives should want to buy into the aesthetic. Such ranges, however, are little more than kitchens in fancy dress. The heart and soul of the vernacular aesthetic is something more elemental, and is not readily available off the peg.

FAR LEFT: The kitchen forms the heart of this sixteenth-century Tuscan farmhouse. The huge open fireplace is clad in travertine from a nearby quarry; the terrazzo flooring, common in many rustic Italian homes, is a more recent feature. **LEFT:** Handmade and handglazed Moroccan tiles provide a vivid backdrop in this Brussels kitchen. The irregularity and randomness that arises from the craft process gives the tiled surface tremendous vitality.

LEFT: A taste for simplicity is a hallmark of vernacular kitchens. Here Yorkstone and metal shelves support African bowls.

BELOW, LEFT TO RIGHT: Traditional Japanese design was the inspiration for this tiny kitchen in a Paris studio. The kitchen is tucked away under a staircase that leads up to a mezzanine level; each stair doubles as a drawer or storage space (left). A sliding rice-paper screen separates the kitchen from the bathroom (centre). Small-scale appliances are tucked away behind MDF doors; a baffle conceals a fluorescent strip lighting the worktop. An internal window brings in natural light (right).

Fitted 'country' kitchens often look a little fake simply because traditional kitchens are generally unfitted. Common features of real traditional kitchens include large wooden tables for eating or preparation, hefty butcher's blocks, plate rails and racks, dressers, deep Belfast sinks, all elements that tend to be assembled piece by piece rather than installed as a single package. And no country kitchen worth its salt is complete without an Aga or old-fashioned cooking range. If the kitchen is the heart of the home, the Aga is the heart of the country kitchen: warm, dependable and decidedly unflashy.

Unfitted kitchens can be compact, but they do work better if there is plenty of room. Better still if you can incorporate the traditional features of the larder and the scullery. A cool north-facing larder with natural ventilation, lined in slate and stone, provides the perfect keeping conditions for a range of produce, from cooked meats and cheeses to stocks of preserves and wine. A scullery, where dishes can be washed and dried out of general view, can help to make the kitchen itself a more pleasant place for eating and general relaxing.

The country kitchen has always put the focus on natural surfaces and finishes, which are rugged and robust rather than sleek and highly finished. Context is also important here; your kitchen will ring true if you can reflect your surroundings and local area in the choice of materials. Stone, brick, terracotta tile and wood will all age sympathetically and weather well.

Colours, too, come from the same natural palette. Chalky whitewash is an unbeatable background. For a warmer, cosier feeling, natural or neutral shades of buff, biscuit and cream, deepening to terracotta, complement natural textures very well, while fresher combinations of blue and white have an appealing domesticity and link the modern kitchen with the past.

Country kitchens have long been synonymous with cheerful clutter: dressers choc-a-bloc with patterned plates and platters; utensils and pots and pans hanging from racks; fresh produce piled in appetising displays. There is no doubt that this type of kitchen holds great appeal for those who like to spend hours rummaging through secondhand shops and market stalls for old-fashioned kitchenalia. At the same time, a more contemporary vernacular look can be achieved by shedding some of the visual busyness in favour of a more spare simplicity founded in the elemental contrasts of different surfaces and textures.

Morocco to Mexico

With mass travel to far-flung corners of the globe, our culinary influences are infinitely broader today than they have ever been. Indeed, many people's idea of traditional food is not the traditional food of their own country, but those simple robust dishes and intense flavours they have encountered while far away from home. Increasingly, as evidenced by the exotic produce now regularly stocked by most supermarkets, once people get a taste for Greek, Thai, Tuscan, Moroccan, Mexican, Indian or Japanese cuisine, they then want to be able to reproduce the full sensory experience in their own kitchens.

A more exotic take on kitchen vernacular draws inspiration from traditional kitchens around the world, such as those one might have come across on holiday. As with the country kitchen aesthetic, these vernacular styles run the risk of looking like 'themed' kitchens once transplanted on home turf: just because you have enjoyed the odd fortnight in Tuscany or Tangiers, it doesn't necessarily follow that your kitchen needs to be fully kitted out in a simulation of 'rustic Italian' or 'Moorish' style – what one might term as souvenir. On the other hand, it is perfectly natural to reflect an affection and appreciation for a particular cuisine by adopting elements of that region's traditions in your kitchen decor. Even better if you like to cook in that style: an Eastern-influenced kitchen, for example, makes perfect sense if your favourite utensil is a wok and five-spice powder regularly features on your shopping list.

Rather than carry out a wholesale makeover, the popular kit-of-parts approach adopted by television decorating programmes, it's far better to suggest an exotic influence

FAR LEFT: The elemental quality of basic surfaces and materials is part of the vernacular appeal, as shown in this vaulted kitchen with walls and ceiling made of rubble stone. LEFT: A variation on the theme of the traditional country dresser, these glass shelves set over a scrubbed pine table provide plenty of space for a comforting display of kitchen clutter. BELOW: Vernacular kitchens tend to include unfitted elements such as the butcher's block. RIGHT: An easy blend of old and new, this unpretentious kitchen features open shelves and racks of crockery, an old painted table and a set of 1950s diner chairs.

more subtly, relying on simply colour and choice of materials to get the message across. Plain, all-white decorative schemes, luminous, airy and cool, evoke unpretentious hot country living, while more intense colours, such as aquamarine, indigo, orange and bright yellow used in luminous washes or glazes have all the *joie de vivre* both of more demonstrative, far-flung cultures and hotter, spicier dishes. Exuberant tilework and vividly coloured ceramics suggest a Spanish influence, rice-paper screens, dark wood and bamboo reflect Far East culture, while raw plaster walls and terracotta tiling call to mind rustic farmhouses of southern Europe.

The underlying appeal of these vernacular traditions, wherever they hail from, lies in the fact that they convey the simple pleasure of food. This directness, of both cooking and presentation, serves as an essential antidote to our increasingly pre-packaged lives.

THE PROFESSIONAL KITCHEN

Over the last ten years or so, the professional kitchen has become an important point of reference for serious home cooks. With more people choosing to socialise in restaurants and with the increased visibility – indeed fame – of chefs, it's not surprising that the boundaries have become blurred between the domestic and professional spheres. Intense mass media interest in cooking and cooks has only accelerated the trend. After Delia Smith mentioned a particular brand of omelette pan in passing on one of her programmes, the manufacturer was so swamped with orders that they had to take on extra staff. If we can't always manage to cook with Delia's reliability or Marco Pierre White's flair, it seems we all want to cook with the same 'professional' kit.

For most domestic cooks, the fully fledged professional kitchen is far from a necessity. Even if you pride yourself on your culinary skills and regularly entertain hordes of friends to three-course meals, you are never going to have to produce the sheer quantity and variety of dishes that emerge from the average restaurant kitchen on a nightly basis. Real professional cooking in any halfway ambitious establishment is cooking under extreme pressure in extreme conditions – it's routinely hot, frantic, exhausting, and occasionally dangerous. However daunted you might be at the prospect of cooking for a dinner party, the task pales by comparison with the frenetic activity of a restaurant kitchen in full swing, where dozens of different orders arrive simultaneously, each requiring different ingredients and techniques to execute. Behind-the-scenes accounts of kitchen life, as described by Anthony Bourdain in *Kitchen Confidential* or Andrew Parkinson in *Cutting It Fine*, portray a world of frayed tempers and phenomenal mental and physical effort far removed from the glamorous milieu of the celebrity television chef.

What can you learn from the professionals? Although the professional kitchen does flatter the aspirations of the wannabe cook, there are certain fundamental principles that are relevant whatever your level of skill. To begin with, the professional kitchen is fitted and equipped to take an enormous amount of punishment; if you choose similar surfaces and fixtures, you'll at least be investing in a kitchen which has the potential to last a lifetime. Cooks also select their utensils with care – they may not own or use a huge range of knives, for example, but they know which knife will best perform any given task and how to keep it in top condition. But, lastly, and most importantly, good professional kitchens are organised for maximum efficiency. In a professional kitchen, wasted effort is wasted time (and money). Applying these principles won't turn you into a starred chef overnight, but you may well find yourself working much more enjoyably and effectively.

Fittings and fixtures

Stainless steel is a material that is virtually synonymous with the professional kitchen. No-nonsense, incredibly robust and with an aura of factory-style precision, stainless steel can be used to clad kitchen surfaces and is often the preferred finish for heavy-duty appliances, fridges and ranges as well. In the true professional kitchen, stainless steel has obvious advantages: it's hygienic, rust-proof, strong and can take a high degree of wear and tear. At home, such qualities are no less welcome, but these advantages must be offset against a relatively high price tag. Maintenance is not entirely trouble-free, either; to preserve the gleaming appearance of stainless steel requires a fair amount of elbow grease and a good proprietary cleaner, such as the type bartenders use to polish their counters to a high shine. If you can't afford stainless steel kitchen units but like the look, basic wooden units can be dressed up with stainless steel panels.

Glass is another modern material with a professional edge. Toughened glass shelves at upper level, glass-fronted fridges or glass splashbacks have a crisp modernity in

RIGHT: The professional kitchen, equipped with individual catering units and industrial fittings and fixtures, has become a reference point for serious cooks.

keeping with the aesthetic. On the floor, pale ceramic tiles, linoleum or similar materials which are unobtrusive and easy to keep clean, strike the right note of efficiency.

Unlike the vernacular kitchen, which is chiefly an unfitted look, the professional kitchen is fundamentally fitted in style. Streamlined, neatly detailed for minimal visual distraction and easy maintenance, and with unit interiors customised with adjustable shelves and pull-out racks, this is the kitchen as a serious working machine. All this puts the emphasis on careful planning to maximise available space and ensure

that working sequences operate in a logical, seamless flow. In *Kitchen Confidential*, Anthony Bourdain repeatedly praises cooks for their 'moves'; a good team of cooks in a busy kitchen do often appear choreographed, displaying an economy of movement and an almost balletic intuition of how to carry through complex and fast-moving sequences without treading on each other's toes. At home, while the need for such finesse is obviously far less acute, tight planning can contribute enormously to the ease of daily and time-efficient kitchen use.

LEFT: A huge ducting vent provides a means of extraction over a long, stainless steel kitchen workbench. The hard-edged aesthetic works particularly well in lofts and other industrial or commercial conversions. **INSET LEFT:** A seductive array of professional kitchen equipment. Every cook can benefit from a decent set of knives and a few robust pans. **ABOVE:** The industrial style of the sleek, sculptural units is tempered by the natural light that pours through two walls of windows. A mobile wheeled unit provides extra storage and preparation space.

One common feature of the professional-style kitchen is the island unit, used as an additional preparation area or as a cooking zone. The island arrangement echoes the typical plan of many restaurant kitchens, where the 'piano' or cooking range forms the focus of the working area. Free-standing 'work benches', which combine sink, hob and worktop in one versatile unit, provide an unfitted variation.

Although the essential nature of the professional kitchen is fitted, with equipment neatly stowed out of the way behind cupboard doors, an element of open storage near the working area is a positive asset. Hanging racks for the *batterie de cuisine*, overhead steel or glass shelves for the pots in constant use, and an arrangement of essential condiments and basic ingredients transform cooking into a smooth operation, where reaching for the salt or the sieve is as instinctive as reaching for the gearshift when you're driving a car. There's no prescribed formula: how you arrange matters will depend on the way you cook and what you like to cook.

Professional kit

At least half the reason why people become enamoured of the professional kitchen is the sheer seductiveness of non-domestic kitchen equipment. It's not just the chefs' knives and catering-sized pots and pans; increasingly, it's also professional-style toasters, blenders, coffee grinders...Not so long ago, if you wanted catering-style equipment you would have had to visit a supplier specialising in equipment for the trade; nowadays, most kitchen departments stock a full range of professional kitchen products.

Professional cooking ranges have become increasingly popular in recent years. These ranges are serious pieces of equipment, built to withstand considerable battering; many are also seriously expensive. It used to be said that the oven door of a range had to be strong enough to support a man's weight, since standing on the door to clean the ventilation hood was common practice at the end of many kitchen shifts. Needless to say, such robustness is far from essential on the domestic front.

If you yearn for the real thing, but baulk at the price tag, a good alternative is to source professional fittings and appliances secondhand. There is nothing down-at-heel or compromised about such a strategy. Because most catering equipment is so robust (and so easy to keep clean) – and because such a huge proportion of new restaurants fail and find themselves forced to close their doors after an embarrassingly short period of time – the trade in second-hand kitchen fittings is healthy and brisk. You may well pick up a bargain with many serviceable years left to go, for a fraction of what you would pay for the same piece of equipment new.

Professional-quality basic equipment – such as knives and pots and pans – do more than earn their keep. (For a full discussion on the merits of various types, see Fittings and Appliances, pages 194–197). In this context, it is enough to say that it is certainly worth investing in good basic utensils that have the potential to last a lifetime with proper care and maintenance: decent, heavy pans that conduct heat properly, generous cast-iron casseroles and a few knives that can be honed to a razor-sharp edge are professional tools that should be in everyone's kitchen.

Over and above the basics, how you equip your kitchen should relate directly to what you like to cook. No serious chef would put up with a pasta-maker occupying valuable counter-space when it was only used half a dozen times a year. If you can't resist impulse buys, at least store your purchases well away from the action.

In many respects, the professional kitchen is a state of mind, a way of organising yourself so that you work at your most effective. For professional cooks, the 'mise-en-place' is an arrangement of basic ingredients – such as salt, pepper, oil and fresh herbs – that they use every shift to create their dishes. Each cook will have a different mise-en-place, according to what they cook, and a different way of arranging it, according to the way they cook and what feels right to them. Setting up and equipping a professional-style kitchen is less about importing status symbols and more about adopting an organised way of thinking.

ABOVE: Acid-green walls set off a selection of professional units and catering equipment, acquired secondhand. **ABOVE RIGHT:** Professional kit is remarkably robust, designed to take considerable punishment. **RIGHT:** The kitchen as food production line. Robust open shelving and plenty of stainless steel convey a no-nonsense approach to cooking.

INDOORS AND OUT

Some of the most memorable and pleasurable experiences of eating – and cooking – happen outdoors. Whether it is a family barbecue on a warm summer's evening, a long, leisurely lunch on a vine-shaded terrace overlooking the sea, or a cook-out on the beach, food always seems to taste better in the open air. It is small wonder that many people's dream kitchen is one that offers an easy connection between indoor and outdoor spaces.

At least part of the appeal of eating and cooking outdoors is the sense of informality. Outdoor cooking, in particular, is cooking at its most direct and unpretentious – no complicated sauces simmering for hours, simply the basic satisfaction of grilling quickly over high heat and transferring the result straight to the plate. Even better if some of the ingredients and flavours can be picked from your own garden; the smallest urban patch can still support a couple of pots of herbs or a modest crop of tomatoes.

When you are considering how to merge kitchen with garden, it is important to look at the whole issue from both sides so that both indoor and outdoor spaces are conceived as a complementary whole. Sightlines, from vantage points both indoors and out, are important, as is consistency of surfaces and finishes.

Making the connection

Kitchens at ground-floor or semi-basement level obviously offer the greatest potential. But even kitchens located on the upper floors can provide some scope for open-air cooking and eating.

The simplest way to merge indoor with outdoor spaces is to improve the means of access to the garden. For ground-floor kitchens this may mean installing French doors in place of a single door, glazing an end wall, enlarging a window or similar straightforward alterations to bring the outdoors more sharply into view. To enhance the sense of connection, you might consider extending the same type of flooring (or at least the same tone of flooring) from indoors to out: wooden floorboards giving way to a decked

On upper levels, a roof terrace or balcony can provide enough space to enjoy the pleasures of outdoor eating whenever the weather permits. The inset wall panel, grouping the light controls, is a neat detail.

ABOVE: A wrap-around verandah that is immediately accessible from the kitchen offers a place to enjoy food amid spectacular scenery. **LEFT:** A stone counter running the entire length of a kitchen and extending right into the garden blurs the distinction between indoors and out. **RIGHT:** Windows that lift right up like hatches can instantly transform the kitchen into an outdoor room – when the weather allows. The primary cooking area, comprising barbecue and cooktop, is located outside under the deck awning. **FAR RIGHT:** The kitchen in this beachside house leads directly to a shaded terrace. Cabinet doors are made of MDF, lacquered silver and yellow using car paint.

area, for example, or pale stone or tile repeated on both sides of the boundary between indoors and out. Similarly, it can be particularly effective to extend a worktop out into the garden so that it forms a continuous work surface.

Most conventional connections with outdoor areas involve a metal or wooden framework to support glazing or glazed doors. It costs a little more and takes a little more design expertise, but reducing such frameworks to a bare minimum, so that the entire wall dividing kitchen from garden effectively reads as an uninterrupted plane of glass, brings the natural world that bit closer.

Extending the kitchen can also provide the opportunity to improve the relationship with outdoor areas. Many terraced city houses have a side passage between the house wall and the neighbouring property which is often unusable as outdoor space. Here, it can make sense to redesign the kitchen to absorb this area; toplighting, skylights or glazed walls will reinforce the connection with the garden without any significant loss of outdoor space. Simple glazed additions to kitchens are another very effective way of merging indoors with out. Developments in glass technology mean that glazed expanses no longer need to be problematic: new techniques for jointing avoid the risk of leaks; new types of glass, such as 'Low E' or low-emissivity glass, prevent excessive heat loss in cold weather. If you don't want to remain on full view the entire time, you could opt for photovoltaic glass which allows you to change the glass from transparent to translucent or opaque at the flick of a switch. Panels of coloured glass add vibrancy and delight.

Top glazing, roof lights and skylights are equally ways of providing kitchens at upper levels with some notional sense of connection with the world outside. Depending on the structure of your home, you might also consider creating a roof garden or top-level conservatory adjacent to a kitchen or eating area. At the very least, a balcony which is large enough for a couple of chairs and a table and a few pots can add a sense of openness to an enclosed kitchen area.

The outdoor kitchen

For those of us who live in temperate regions of the world, cooking outdoors is not a year-round option. But if you enjoy eating and cooking al fresco, it makes sense to set up and equip an outdoor cooking/eating area so you can take advantage of any spell of fine weather whenever it occurs.

Outdoor cooking tends to mean some form of grilling. There is a huge range of barbecues on the market, from basic, hibachi-style disposable trays to massive affairs complete with built-in rotisseries; a popular option, which falls somewhere between such extremes, is the type of drum or lidded bowl barbecue on a wheeled stand which concentrates heat so that food cooks evenly and efficiently all through. Built-in barbecues or grills are not difficult to construct; site such features where smoke will not blow indoors but sufficiently close to the kitchen to make preparation and cooking more straightforward. If you do opt for a built-in arrangement, you should also provide space around the grill for setting down plates and platters.

If you're cooking outside, chances are you'll want to eat outside as well. An outdoor eating area can be as impromptu as a blanket spread over the grass; tables and chairs, however, turn the garden into a true outdoor room.

Simple, robust garden furniture can be surprisingly difficult to track down; the market tends to be dominated by fancy wrought-ironwork in pastiche Victoriana at one extreme and flimsy plastic at the other. Look for canvas director's chairs, plain folding café chairs in slatted wood and metal, basic hardwood benches and tables that weather to an attractive patina, or Lloyd Loom-style basket chairs for greater comfort. There's no need for garden furniture to differ fundamentally in style from furniture indoors: tables and chairs that are light enough to move indoors and out as need and weather dictate are one solution.

Set up an eating area where there is a level surface and where there is an attractive viewpoint and remember to provide shade with an awning, pergola or trellis. Artificial garden lighting, in the form of flares, candles, lanterns or fairy lights, adds a magical dimension to evening meals.

As supermarket produce becomes ever more bland and insipid, merging indoors with out provides the chance to grow your own fresh fruit, vegetables and herbs. In days gone by, the kitchen garden was the essential adjunct to every country house, no matter how modest in size. With food scares constantly hitting the headlines and the growth of interest in organic methods of production, the time is ripe for a revival of these traditional skills. Container-grown herbs could not be simpler or more foolproof; basic salad vegetables such as lettuces and tomatoes demand little expertise. Flavour is fugitive: growing your own cuts the distance between plot and plate to an absolute minimum, maximising freshness and taste.

RIGHT: An electronically controlled glass roof slides back to create a sunny open-air eating area. Low-emissivity glass and underfloor heating help to maintain a comfortable indoor temperature on less clement days. **BELOW LEFT:** This outdoor cooking and eating area is simplicity itself, with the slatted structure that houses the preparation area echoing the expanse of timber decking. **BELOW RIGHT:** Food tastes better outdoors, particularly cooked in a wood-fired oven. **BELOW FAR RIGHT:** An indoor/outdoor kitchen and preparation area cuts the time from pan to plate. The stoves are set into a worktop made of waxed cement.

case study: THE INDOOR/OUTDOOR KITCHEN

Running the full width of the house, this large, light-filled kitchen merges almost seamlessly with the decked outdoor area and garden. When the owners, Winfried Heinze and his partner Heather, bought the property they knew immediately how they wanted it changed. Their previous home had been a tall, narrow terraced house with limited spatial possibilities. In this house, the greater width made it possible to open out the ground floor completely and fully connect with the outside areas. The kitchen was conceived as the central focus of the house and the intention was to make it big enough so that all other activities could happen around it.

ABOVE: The garden is also a productive space – herbs are grown near the house for easy access. **RIGHT:** At the bottom of the garden is a patch where Winfried and Heather grow berries, tomatoes and salad vegetables. **ABOVE RIGHT:** Looking through the kitchen to the garden. Glazed doors fill the end wall. A floor-level heating channel runs along at the base of the doors so that radiators do not interrupt the space.

Unusually, Winfried and Heather ran the entire scheme themselves, from design to project management, using an architect only to gain the necessary building permissions and sourcing many of the materials and fittings on the internet. The house was stripped back to its bare bones, with most internal walls removed to create a big open space. The glazed end walls, fitted with sliding doors, mean that from any point on the ground floor the entire garden is visible. The airy, spacious quality is a positive advantage for Winfried, a photographer who sometimes works from home.

LEFT AND ABOVE: The sleek centrepiece of the kitchen is a stainless steel island, made to the owners' specification by a manufacturer who produces kitchen fittings for professional applications. The island houses a hob and oven; the fridge and ventilation unit were sourced on the internet, which resulted in considerable savings. **RIGHT:** View from the garden into the kitchen. While work was being carried out on the house, Winfried and Heather rented a flat nearby, so that daily progress could be closely monitored. The key practical challenge was coordinating the sequence of work.

LEFT: The end wall is filled with four sliding glass doors; the two outer doors slide over the middle pair, leaving a protected zone in the centre of the space. This arrangement means that on cooler days people can sit indoors with the doors open without feeling a chill. Indoors the flooring is grey Spanish limestone in large square slabs; outdoors the decking is in ipe, a Brazilian hardwood. The modern dining table, made by a friend, is walnut on an aluminium frame and legs.

RIGHT: Detail of the stainless steel shelving on one side of the kitchen island. BELOW: Fitted units provide storage in the kitchen area, supplemented by tall glass-fronted cupboards for crockery and glassware.

Basic Elements

Work surfaces, flooring, wall treatments and lighting are the basic elements that will instil a sense of character into your kitchen and, at the same time, help achieve a practical, hardworking room for all your activities. When it comes to making decisions about the choice of surfaces, finishes and fixtures for your kitchen, it is important to consider both style and efficiency. Will a timber worktop better suit your needs than a light-up glass version? What type of storage do you prefer? And if you have children are smudge-prone, stainless steel door fronts really the best option?

These considerations do not mean, however, that practicality should be achieved at the expense of a pleasant and stylish working environment. There can be nothing worse than an unloved, utilitarian kitchen which is bland and dull to be in, and it is possible to combine function with individuality.

Today there is a wealth of materials and fittings adopted for kitchen use. Some hold traditional associations with the kitchen (wood, stone and ceramic, for instance) while others like rubber, glass and steel have winged their way from the restaurant world or techno industry into our homes. All offer a variety of advantages, and will suit different applications, lifestyles and budgets.

Such a diverse selection can be both attractive and bewildering at the same time, so the aim of this chapter is to provide you with all the information you need to choose these basic essentials.

ABOVE: Mixing materials is a good way of adding design interest. Dark teak worktops and splashbacks are offset by the white sink, maple cabinets and stainless steel door. **LEFT:** Contrasting floor materials define different zones. The working area features a blue mosaic floor in contrast to the warmer stripped floorboards in the dining section. An unbroken wall of mosaics throughout unifies the space. **RIGHT:** A raw, sculptural island unit has been fashioned from concrete and appears to rise seamlessly from the concrete tiled flooring. The long wooden table was constructed from two old garden pine trees which fell down during a hurricane.

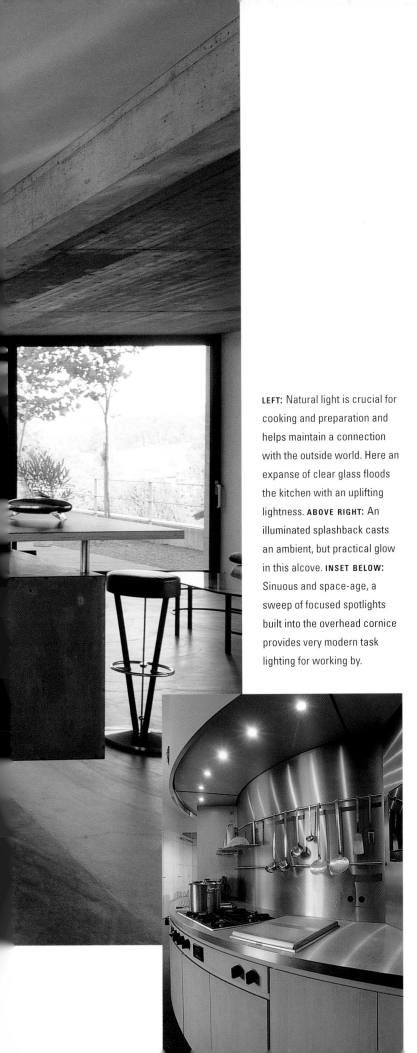

LEFT: Natural light is crucial for cooking and preparation and helps maintain a connection with the outside world. Here an expanse of clear glass floods the kitchen with an uplifting lightness. **ABOVE RIGHT:** An illuminated splashback casts an ambient, but practical glow in this alcove. **INSET BELOW:** Sinuous and space-age, a sweep of focused spotlights built into the overhead cornice provides very modern task lighting for working by.

LIGHTING

Now that kitchens have become the multifunctional hub of the home – somewhere to cook, eat and relax – it is important to invest in flexible lighting that can cope with every scenario. Before you choose a lighting system, think about how you use your kitchen. Look at how much natural light the room gets by noting the number of windows and which way they face and how the light differs at different times of the day and year; then work out how this can be enhanced with artificial lighting. The colours, textures and materials you choose for worktops, splashbacks and cupboard doors will also affect the quality of light. Pale colours reflect light and dark colours absorb it. If your kitchen is made up of richly stained wood units and slate floor tiles, you will need to maximise the light by allocating extra, brighter bulbs. Matt finishes, such as sandblasted aluminium, diffuse light, while high-gloss surfaces and stainless steel pick up reflections, causing glare – this can be minimised by using a frosted lens and adding dimmer switches.

Remember to plan well in advance, as last-minute lighting schemes can limit options and cause disruption and extra cost at a later date. You may want to seek advice from a lighting expert or interior designer who will have an understanding of the different sources of light, as well as their direction and control. Always employ a qualified electrician to ensure a safe and well-fitted installation.

Kitchen lighting divides into two types: task lighting to cook and prepare food by, and ambient lighting for everyday use and for dining and relaxing by.

Task lighting

First and foremost, the kitchen is a hardworking room, so practical needs must be addressed at the outset. Light sources should always be in front of you, rather than behind, to prevent your shadow coming between you and the task you are working on.

Bright, efficient task lighting is essential for the hard-working element of your kitchen, for preparation, cooking and washing up. Under-cupboard lighting directed over the hob, sink and chopping board will provide focused task lighting. Position lights as close to the front edge of the cupboard as possible, otherwise you will illuminate the back of the worktop rather than the activity you are working on. Low-voltage halogen gives a bright, crisp light and bulbs are slim enough to recess into the base of cupboards. Strip lighting can also be mounted on the underside of cupboards or shelves and be fitted with a baffle or reflector to subdue glare. For island units where there are no wall cupboards to affix the light fitting, choose ceiling-mounted downlighters with the right beam width to create focused light. Most extractor hoods now come with built-in lighting to illuminate the hob while cookers are usually equipped with interior lights. Sinks need light reflected directly on to bowls and draining boards. Wherever possible, fit automatic lights to the inside of storage cupboards that will turn on and off as the door opens and shuts.

Ambient lighting

Effective ambient or general lighting will help create different moods. If you have an open-plan kitchen, you will need a versatile scheme with subtle, mood lighting as well as bright lights to merge in with the rest of the space. A single or row of dimmable pendants above a table will create an intimate light for eating and help differentiate the dining space from the kitchen's work zones. A rise-and-fall fixture can be pulled down for a cosy candlelit supper or raised for everyday meals and other activities.

The layout and size of your kitchen will dictate the number and arrangement of lights. Take time to position them correctly as lights placed in the centre of the room will focus on the floor rather than the perimeter of the room where most of the working kitchen is sited. Track lights and spotlights will wash the walls and surfaces with light while a series of recessed halogens will be less of an obstruction in kitchens with low ceilings. And don't forget exposed fittings will collect cooking grime and grease more readily than recessed or semi-recessed lights set flush into a surface. Lights positioned on top of wall units or wall-mounted uplighters will have the effect of raising the ceiling and create good general lighting at the same time.

Coloured lighting

Many hotels and restaurants are experimenting with coloured lighting, not only as a way to alter a room's appearance but also as a way to affect the mood of the people who are in it. The idea is based on the principle that colours stimulate the brain in different ways, for example, indigo for clear thinking and concentration, green for forgiveness and acceptance, and orange for passion and vitality. This type of ambient lighting is more suited to the relaxation zones of the house, but could be used to a limited extent in the kitchen as a dramatic mood-making device. Coloured light is not advisable for task lighting.

Types of light

▸ Tungsten or incandescent bulbs are cheap, readily available and easy to use and replace. They come in various styles, colours and wattages and create a warm, mellow light, which resembles natural light more closely than fluorescent tubes. However, around 90 per cent of the energy is converted into heat, not light, so they are not suitable for use near flammable materials. Tungsten bulbs have the shortest lifespan (up to 1,000 hours) so offset the cost by turning the lights down when you aren't preparing food and turn them off when you're not in the kitchen.

▸ Halogen bulbs emit a whiter, crisper light. They are also much smaller, and ideal for adding light unobtrusively, for example, as recessed downlighters built into a ceiling. The lamp is filled with halogen gas within which the filament burns. It has a quartz body instead of glass, allowing the halogen lamps to reach much higher temperatures – the light is literally 'white hot', so do not install at low level or where hands may come into contact with it. Low-voltage halogen bulbs are even more compact with a lower wattage and are operated via a transformer, as opposed to mains operation. Dichroic halogen lights were developed for the food industry so that the kitchens did not become too hot for the chefs. A special dichroic coating that stops infrared light from passing beyond the bulb means that they radiate a cool beam. Halogen also lasts considerably longer than

FAR LEFT: One-space living requires a variety of lights to accommodate different needs. A row of pendant lights over the dining table creates a more intimate light for eating and sets it apart from the cooking area where directional spotlights are employed. **LEFT:** Recessed downlighters make a feature out of this narrow aperture and add extra illumination at the same time. **ABOVE:** Skylights are an effective way of punching natural light into a dark, narrow kitchen but remember to complement with good artificial lighting. Here a large suspended striplight has been installed for evenings and dark mornings.

tungsten (up to 3,000 hours) though the amount of energy used to generate light is more or less the same. Bulbs are fragile and require special handling with a clean cotton cloth as any oil from your fingertips may damage the bulb.

▶ Fluorescent tube lighting is very bright and powerful and should be well baffled and not looked at directly. It used to have a reputation for harsh, flickering light, although this has been improved with newer (and more expensive) dimmable versions. Compact fluorescents are thin tubes that can be folded and enclosed within a pearl bulb for a warmer light. Fluorescents are extremely energy efficient (lasting up to 8,000 hours) with a low-heat emission – an undoubted benefit in a room of heat-generating equipment.

▶ Fibre optic lighting can create a magical, starry ambience. Light is shone down thin strands of coated fibreglass or acrylic, where it emerges only at the ends. This allows the light source to be placed some distance from the light that is emitted, making it cool at point of delivery. Strands can be touched, bent or used underwater; in the kitchen fibre optically lit glass worktops or fibre optic carpets will add an individual touch. However, it is expensive and comes with a bulky light-source box.

▶ LED (or light-emitting diodes) are the small red lights used in watches and stereos. They are fairly uncommon for the domestic scene, but they are extremely energy efficient (with a 100,000-hour lamp life) and have a very low heat emission. As such, they are ideal for areas that are awkward to replace, such as recessed floor uplighters.

Light fittings

Whether you opt for sleek, modern styles or a more traditional, period look, your choice of light fitting will determine the effect. The common denominator here is that all kitchen lights must suit their assigned task, be easy to clean and have easily replaceable bulbs or tubes.

▶ Track lighting is most flexible in its 'free form' version where different lights can be fitted at any point along the track and moved about. This allows you to create a lighting system personalised for your needs, for example, spotlights

ABOVE: Here, the conventional splashbacks are ingeniously replaced by narrow, sliding windows to allow fresh air and natural light into a confined space. **ABOVE RIGHT:** A row of green glass pendants provides even illumination over the work surface when natural light fails.

BELOW RIGHT: Natural light has been enhanced as much as possible in this top-floor kitchen by the installation of large windows and a ceiling made of flat panes of glass. In addition to this, a section of glass bricks in the floor allows light to filter in from downstairs.

at the working end of the kitchen and a pendant in the dining area. The more reasonably priced 'fixed' track usually has around four permanent light fittings, which cannot be repositioned. Track can be mounted vertically or horizontally, on the wall and ceiling. However, it can be intrusive and also reminiscent of a shop's display lighting and is only suitable for modern kitchens.

▸ Downlighters can be recessed or semi-recessed into the ceiling or under cupboards to provide effective task lighting. They are dimmable and come in different beam widths. Directional downlighters are even more flexible.

▸ Spotlights use incandescent reflector bulbs that are silvered on the inside, or low-voltage halogen. They can be fitted on to a track system or directly on to a surface.

▸ Wall lights and wall washers create a subtle form of background light. They are good for creating mood lighting for areas meant for eating and relaxing.

Control systems

Dimmer switches are an excellent way of creating a soft, ambient glow for dining in the kitchen. They reduce the amount of light by decreasing power to the light source, extending the life of the lamp at the same time. Dimmers are available as rotary/push button, touch control and remote control versions. For the ultimate scene-setting device, intelligent light systems allow you to create and then recall pre-set light patterns at the touch of the button. You can also pre-set lighting to switch on or off at certain times and to respond to changes in natural light levels.

Switches

Stick to simple, unfussy switches in wipeable materials such as plastic, brushed nickel, Perspex and chrome. Install them at elbow height, so even if your hands are full they can be flicked on or off with relative ease. If the kitchen is large and has more than one entrance, each lighting area should have its own switch so it can be controlled separately. This offers maximum flexibility and economy, allowing you to illuminate just one half of the kitchen at a time.

WALLS

As with any room, kitchen walls come alive with colour and texture. A kitchen with plain-fronted, blonde wood doors may benefit from a solid block of bright colour or a band of shiny glass mosaics. On the other hand, kitchen cupboards that make a statement of their own, either with a strong colour or an unusual wood grain, will probably suit a more neutral backdrop.

Colour and decoration aside, kitchen walls need to be practical and hardwearing. No other room in the house is bombarded with the same combination of wet and dry heat, dust, fats and oils. Smooth finishes are far better in a busy kitchen – a textured surface with too many undulations will be harder to wipe clean.

Material choices

Paint This is a brilliantly simple way to add colour to kitchen walls and surfaces. Blackboard paint can be used to create a smooth, hardwearing writing surface. Choosing a colour scheme from a colour card is difficult, so it is always wise to buy sample pots first for accuracy and also to look at the colour at different times of the day.

The hot, humid conditions of a kitchen call for a durable paint finish. Oil-based eggshell is a good choice, as it creates a semi-sheen finish that can be wiped down easily. Silk emulsion is another; it is a tough and washable water-based paint with a hardwearing and scuff-resistant silky finish and can be bought with various sheens: from shiny to satin to an almost matt look and feel. Matt emulsion is less durable

LEFT: Bare plaster painted a rich, deep shade of brown adds a rugged, natural touch. Colourful kitchen paraphernalia hung on a simple chain are all the colour that is needed. RIGHT: Metro-style white tiles are clean and hardwearing and completely at home in this modern country kitchen. BELOW RIGHT: Exposing the original brickwork on one wall retains a sense of character in this warehouse conversion, while stainless steel worktops bring the look completely up to date.

and is better suited to kitchen ceilings. Many stores now sell paints specifically designed for the damp, moist conditions of kitchens. They have a soft sheen finish that is moisture-resistant, tough and durable, and easy to wipe.

Good preparation will add years to your paintwork. Use sugar soap and water to wash down all surfaces, starting with the ceiling, and allow to dry before painting. If there are any damp patches, find the cause and remedy it. When dry, coat with a primer/sealer. Plaster surfaces with nicotine stains also need to be coated with primer/sealer. Older houses may have a coating of distemper. Wash and scrape off as much of it as possible and cover with stabilising solution before repainting. Any cracks and holes should be filled and then lightly sanded, prior to the main coat.

Plaster Bare plaster is a very durable and inexpensive finish. If you plan to paint the surface, the plaster needs to be primed first with a diluted coat of emulsion. You can create depth and character on plaster by working in powdered paint for a marbled effect. Alternatively, several coats of tinted limewash will build up a soft, chalky bloom of colour while the addition of metallic dust will create a sparkling surface. A water-based waxy glaze will add subtle shading, but remember to seal it with a coat of matt varnish for a hardwearing surface.

ABOVE LEFT: Glass bricks allow light to filter in subtly from an adjoining room, creating a softer division than a solid wall would, and intensifying the colour of the bright units and ergonomic curves. **TOP:** Simple tongue-and-groove panelling in a muted olive green creates a distinct Shaker feel – a warm and welcoming setting where the natural hues of herbs and spices are the best form of decoration. The uniformly spaced jars provide a visual contrast to the vertical lines of the panelling. **ABOVE:** A wall of bold paintwork enlivens the blocky, freestanding steel units and task lamps.

Tiles Hardwearing and water-resistant, ceramic tiles are ideal for kitchen walls. They are made from clay fired at very high temperatures to strengthen them and come in a wide choice of size, colour and design. Handpainted decorative tiles and colourwashed crackle glaze tiles look effective in older houses while steel-effect tiles with stud and grille textures will add an industrial edge to any kitchen. Specialist companies can create one-off designs and colours to order; alternatively search for antique tiles from old houses or salvage yards. You can also commission digitally printed ceramic tiles with your own design or image. Vitrified tiles have a low water absorption (between 0.5 and 3 per cent) and are more dense and durable than earthenware tiles. Most floor tiles are vitrified although glazed vitrified wall and cladding tiles are becoming increasingly popular.

Wall tiles are subject to less wear than floors, so are thinner; they are also easier to work with and cut or snap to a scored line. Glass mosaics or smooth, matt versions can create a sleek and practical splashback. Remember that all unglazed tiles must be sealed.

Tiles can be stuck to most walls as long as the surface is flat, clean, dry and stable. You can tile on top of old ceramic tiles providing they are clean and degreased but stagger the joint lines away from the old ones for extra strength. Old wallpaper must be removed and gloss-painted walls sanded down to provide a key for the adhesive. Old tiles can be refreshed by simply painting over them. Use a tile primer as a base coat and then brush with a tile gloss for a mirror finish and a brand-new look.

Wallpaper Don't overlook wallpaper. Seek out good-quality vinyl wallpapers, which are moisture-resistant and steam-proof. Wallpaper designs have come on hugely in recent years, and are now available in a range of sophisticated patterns and modern designs including metal-effects, glossy lacquers, even faux-snakeskin. In addition to covering the entire room, it can be used as an accent by putting up one or two panels or printed with a photo mural or image. Tough, textured paper will also disguise uneven walls.

Wood A popular material for the kitchen, wood is most commonly used on worktops, flooring and door fronts. Not only is it a warm, attractive and natural material, it is easy to keep clean with a damp cloth and mild detergent. Wood falls into two basic categories. Hardwoods come from broad-leaved, deciduous trees that shed their leaves in the winter months, such as oak, ash, beech and maple. Softwood is a timber from any coniferous, evergreen tree, for example, pine and spruce, and can be used for wallpapering or ceilings in tongue-and-groove boards.

There are also a wide number of species to choose from. Oak has a rich tone and classic grain; beech is a popular wood in a pale, light tan colour. Beech and oak can also be stained throughout to achieve the rich, tawny look of a tropical timber. Cherry is one of the best woods for the kitchen and will deepen over time into a bronze shade; maple is a straight-grained white wood; and iroko is a solid timber from Africa, similar to teak. It is naturally oily and deepens to a rich brown. Character oak which displays the wood's natural features such as pippy knots, clusters and splits exudes a quintessential English look, perfect for country kitchens, while limed, frosted and bleached oak yields a much lighter, more contemporary finish. Ash, beech, sycamore and maple are blonder woods, and will provide a more neutral backdrop. Tropical woods such as teak, iroko and wenge should always be bought from reclamation or salvage yards. Rare or environmentally protected species should only be bought if they are from sustainably managed forests and new timber from well-managed woodlands. Check with your supplier; although most manufacturers use sustainable forests, it can take over 100 years for an oak tree to reach maturity.

Tongue-and-groove panelling is one of the easiest ways to liven up a kitchen and conceal uneven and crumbling walls. Painted in a cool white or a muted blue or clear varnished, it will bring a distinct Shaker style to the room. Seal timber wall surfaces against damp and stains, and insulate with metal sheets or fireproof material if they are adjacent to the cooker or hob.

case study:
THE MATERIALS KITCHEN

Using contrasting materials on surfaces and finishes is a tried-and-tested way of adding depth of character to a room, but even within the same broad family there can be distinctive variations of tone and texture. In this Manhattan loft kitchen, designed by architects, Moneo Brock, the interplay of different types of wood creates a warm and lively effect. The utilitarian character of the space, expressed in the massive exposed oak beams and pillars, is tempered by smooth painted plaster surfaces and sleek flooring.

LEFT: Douglas fir strip flooring, laid on the diagonal, adds a dynamic quality to the space. The dining table is made of yellow pine; kitchen units are faced in pale birch. The facing panels on the box-like divider enclosing the kitchen area are oriented strandboard, a type of cheap manufactured board more commonly used as temporary boarding for shop fronts. **RIGHT:** A strandboard-faced divider partitions the kitchen from the main loft space. The more sombre grooved draining board and unit tops are made of slate.

WORKTOPS AND SPLASHBACKS

Worktops are probably the hardest-working element of your kitchen, subjected to a daily onslaught of knocks, spills, hot pans, sharp knives and the occasional human being (for who hasn't clambered on to a worktop to change a light bulb or reach the back of cupboards?). Strength and resilience are the greatest priority, but worktops must also be hygienic and easy to wipe clean. The best ones also resist the abrasive effects of scouring and will not absorb the stains from food, vinegar and oil. If possible use one length of worktop, keeping joins and seams to a minimum. This way there will be less of an opportunity for bacteria and dirt to build up in crevices. For similar reasons, sinks should be either flush-fitted or undermounted into the worktop. Select the thickest worktop you can afford. The most common thicknesses are 30mm and 40mm, but a 40mm worktop tends to have greater resistance to heat and damage and is less prone to cracking or warping.

The material you choose will mainly depend on personal preference, style of kitchen and budget, but keen cooks may wish to use more than one worktop material in the same kitchen, specific to an intended activity. For example, an area of smooth, cold marble is ideal for rolling pastry, end-grain maple makes the perfect chopping board while a section of stainless steel around the cooking area will double as a sleek pan rest. Don't overcomplicate the room with too many materials, especially in a small kitchen; alternatively use loose cutting boards, which can be moved from area to area and washed easily.

The splashback is the wall area between the base units and the upper cupboards, and as its name suggests is subject to a daily onslaught of water, grease, steam, liquids and other rogue cooking ingredients. As such, it must be water-resistant and easy to clean. Use a heat-resistant surface such as stainless steel, tile or stone around the cooker or hob and don't overlook the seam between the worktop and the splashback, which is a potential dirt trap and breeding ground. Fill with a special rubber sealant or if you opt for wood, invest in a matching upstand which is fixed between the back edge of the worktop and the wall. Even better use a continuous sheet of material to create a one-piece, seam-free worktop and splashback.

Material choices

Wood Looks aside, wood is also extremely hygienic, and possesses a natural acidity that inhibits bacterial growth (see page 129 for more general information). This makes it a great surface for food preparation, but it is important to treat the wood so the worktop can withstand the heat, moisture and heavy use of a working kitchen. Oiled solid hardwood, such as teak, oak or iroko is probably the best option, as it is most resistant to heat and stains and tends to improve with age. The silky, oiled finish also enhances the colour and grain of the wood and creates a surface that is easy to clean. The worktop will usually come pre-oiled; however, after installation, it should be sanded lightly and given an extra layer of oil for further protection. After the initial treatment, only simple maintenance is required with the occasional re-oiling. Any scratches or discoloration can be removed with fine sandpaper, re-oiled and left to dry. A lacquered wood is not so hardwearing, and hot and cold fluids will eventually break down the lacquer which should be reapplied annually. However, it is more reasonably priced. End-grain wood turned on its end and glued together in blocks or slats gives a very dense surface, ideal for butcher's blocks – maple is a good choice as it won't flavour foods.

If a washing machine or dishwasher is to be installed under a wooden worktop, a moisture barrier is required, which is glued to the underside of the worktop. You must allow a ventilation gap of at least 25mm around appliances and between the ends of freestanding cookers (a minimum of 40mm if you have a range cooker). Remember solid wood works across the grain, so it must be installed to allow expansion and contraction.

RIGHT: Thick slabs of Carrara marble add a further purist's touch to this sleek, uncluttered kitchen, in stark contrast to the abundance of natural foliage outside.

Glass Sheets of toughened 19mm or 25mm glass are extremely resilient, hygienic and easy to clean, and create attractive, modern worktops. The glass is available as transparent, milky or totally opaque in myriad colours including metallic and pearlescent finishes. It can be colour enamelled on the underside and even illuminated with fibre optic lighting, but this can be extremely expensive. Glass does naturally scratch, although glass with a textured underside will 'refract' any scratches on the smooth surface. A finely textured 'orange peel' top layer will disguise any scratches. Toughened glass will shatter safely into millions of tiny pieces, but this type of safety glass cannot withstand large cut-outs for a sink and hob. Non-toughened glass may be a better option and it is still safe, as it has a film applied to the back to hold the shards of glass in place should the worktop shatter. Practically, it is far more flexible, allowing for cut-outs and special edge finishes. Even though non-toughened glass can take temperatures of up to 40°C it is still advisable to use a piece of toughened, heat-resistant glass around the hob area as it may crack if a hot pan is placed on it. Glass is a good option for splashbacks and can be fixed simply with bolts or silicone glue. Much thinner sheets of glass are used, around 10 or 12mm, and can also be back-lit to create a mesmerising glow. Coloured or opaque glass is a good choice if you want to hide uneven plaster or unsightly marks on the wall or you could paint the underside with special glass paint.

Stainless steel An increasingly popular choice for worktops and splashbacks, stainless steel will add a professional edge to your kitchen. Good-quality steel is also hardwearing, hygienic and heat-proof and should be at least 0.9mm thick with an 18/8 grading. Any thinner and the worktop may flex under pressure.

Stainless steel is available in brushed, polished and patterned finishes. Worktops can be fitted with an integral sink, draining board and splashback for a streamlined, seamless finish to minimise the number of joins.

Smudges and fingerprints are an inevitable by-product of usage, but maintenance is simple – wash with water and a mild detergent and polish dry with a soft cloth. A thin coating of baby oil applied with a dry cloth will bring back a sleek sheen to a smeared surface. Stainless steel is also susceptible to scratches, although over time these will meld together into a patina that will reflect the use they have been put to.

Zinc With a greyer, duller, more seductive sheen than stainless steel, zinc is gaining popularity for worktops. Thin sheets of roofing zinc can be glued to a base of MDF and wrapped around and fixed to the front edge. Any joins should be soldered. Zinc does scratch and stain, but this adds to its charm; eventually the worktop will develop a soft burnished patina. Zinc is also heat- and water-resistant and much easier to clean than stainless steel (fingerprints aren't quite as obvious) – it also comes with a cheaper price tag.

Stone Natural stone is an excellent material for worktops, hardwearing and robust with a cool surface ideal for food preparation. There are myriad different colours and textures available and most come in a polished or matt finish. All surfaces except polished granite should be sealed (most are supplied pre-sealed from the factory) and a wipe over with a damp cloth is all the maintenance required. Avoid scouring powders and cream cleaners as they can contain abrasives that may dull the surface.

FAR LEFT: Characterful and well-used, this solid old dresser has a worn wooden top for preparing food. The rustic ambience is complemented by a stainless steel range cooker. **LEFT:** This impressive island unit tempers the sterility of the all-white storage cupboards and vast extractor fan by incorporating a smooth block of pale, silvery wood and turquoise units. **ABOVE LEFT:** An uninterrupted line of stainless steel creates a hygienic and hardwearing work surface. **ABOVE RIGHT:** Milky-green glass splashbacks create subtle colour against a stainless steel surface.

For a stone splashback you will only need a veneer thickness as it does not have to withstand any heavy weight or pressure. Worktops need to be much thicker to create a robust and solid preparation surface, but you should remember that a length of solid stone can be extremely heavy as well as expensive and will require sturdy kitchen units beneath.

GRANITE This is a high-density stone which is extremely hardwearing, and almost impossible to scratch or chip. It is also heatproof (hot pans can be placed directly on the surface), waterproof and difficult to stain, making it a brilliant choice for kitchen worktops. In addition to these attributes, the cool, smooth surface is ideal for food preparation.

Granite is available in a wide range of colours, often with bold natural markings and rich, deep colouring, including green, black and earthy brown. Worktops are cut to size and can be honed to a smooth, matt, eggshell finish. Granite is a crystalline material which is more susceptible to cracking if not adequately supported. If possible, use in a greater thickness or fix to a MDF sub-base.

MARBLE These worktops provide a cold, hard surface, ideal for pastry making. However it can be easily stained by acids such as sugar, alcohol and lemon juice. Some marbles are more dense and less porous than others; always specify a honed finish. Alternatively use an inset slab of marble for kneading and combine with a different material elsewhere.

LIMESTONE This stone tends to come in light, natural tones like honey, buff and pale cream, although rich blue/grey varieties are available. It has subtle textures and natural veining with a smooth, matt finish for even wear and tear. Most limestone is porous and should be protected with multiple layers of sealant to prevent staining and acid erosion. Again, limestone is not really recommended for full worktop use in a hardworking kitchen.

SLATE Less expensive than other stones, slate worktops can create a dramatic look in your kitchen. With a honed, velvety-smooth finish, slate is available in black and deep tones of blue, green and silvery grey. It is hardwearing, resistant to heat and wipes clean with a damp cloth. Make sure you choose a slate with a high silica content and add a protective sealant to reduce the porosity. More porous slates will absorb oils and stain easily. Surface scratches can be removed with gentle sandpapering.

Pyrolave This material is made from volcanic lava stone that has been fired in the earth's own kiln, which means it can withstand the hottest temperatures that a busy domestic kitchen can inflict on it. It has a delicately crazed surface and resembles one large slab of ceramic tile, but without the grouting. Design, colour and texture can be applied to the surface.

Solid surfaces These are also known as composite materials and should not be confused with solid, natural stone. Instead, composites are a man-made, non-porous material, made up of acrylic resins and natural minerals – hence the name 'composite'. The result is an extremely practical worktop which is stain-resistant, waterproof and very durable. It has a smooth, silky surface that is warm to the touch. The colour runs throughout the thickness of the material, making it renewable – any scratches, burns or dents can be gently sanded down and polished to create a new blemish-free surface.

Composites like Corian and Paracor can be cut, carved, routed and sandblasted into any curve or twisted into shape you want, making it a highly desirable choice for complicated design ideas. Sheets of solid surface can be joined without any seams or gaps, creating a sleek worktop, eliminating

ABOVE LEFT: Bright laminate worktops and seamless splashback are not only practical and robust, but also enliven a functional area.
ABOVE RIGHT: Grey stone worktops with an integral, grooved drainer temper the deep aubergine of the cabinet doors. RIGHT: The burnished gleam of zinc has been wrapped around worktops and side panels creating an unusual contrast with the white door fronts. The tangerine cupboard is designed as a solid block of colour. Some of the doors open downwards to double as a desk or worktop space.

dirt and bacteria traps. It can also be combined with an inset solid surface sink (in the same or contrasting colour), a grooved integral drainer or inlaid with steel rods for a built-in pot rest.

The range of colour and pattern available is diverse, from a cool glacier white to a speckled granite-effect to bold blocks of single colour in hot orange and yellow. All solid surface worktops are made to order and must be installed by a professional fabricator which will increase the already high overall price.

Laminates Forget the peeling, dreary and faded laminate worktop that is so reminiscent of the 1970s. These days, laminates are high-quality products and come in an exhaustive palette of colours and finishes such as plain matt tones, convincing woodgrains and subtle patterns to match any style of kitchen. They are extremely reasonably priced and hardwearing, with an easy-to-maintain surface that can also withstand high temperatures and a certain amount of knocks and scratches.

A high-pressure laminate is made up of many layers of coloured or patterned paper impregnated with resins. These are fused under high pressure and heat and covered with a clear melamine overlay – the whole structure is then glued to a chipboard, plywood or MDF substrate. Look for a moisture-resistant backing on the underside that will provide extra protection.

Avoid using harsh and abrasive cleaners that can scratch and dull the finish, while prolonged wetting or flooding may warp the surface of the laminate. Once damaged, laminates usually cannot be easily repaired, seams and marks are fairly hard to disguise and you end up having to replace the surface entirely.

Solid-core laminates are a more hardwearing option, with solid colour running throughout the thickness of the material. They can be used to make thinner worktops than the standard thickness – 20mm as opposed to 40mm – and give a sleeker look. Laminate worktops can be made with a curved edge to get rid of sharp corners.

Tiles Despite their strength and water-resistance, tiles are best used for splashbacks rather than worktops, although vitrified tiles can work well (see page 129 for more information). The tile itself is simple enough to clean but the grouting in between is easily stained with foods, liquid and dirt. Unless you use an epoxy grout or are prepared to re-grout regularly, ceramic tiles are better used to create a striking splashback. They come in a huge choice of size, colour and design, including plain, glossy, matt, metallic and patterned, or try rows of tiny mosaics in glass, ceramic or stone. For ease of use, buy sheets of mosaics mounted on to a mesh backing. Instead of fixing each mosaic individually, the sheets can be cut to size and fixed directly to the wall.

Concrete These worktops add an earthy, textural element to a kitchen. Unlike the concrete used in pavements, a concrete worktop is mixed with additives to make it less susceptible to chipping and cracking. Worktops are usually cast in situ, at your home and on top of existing kitchen

carcases. The top is then ground to a polished surface and treated with a special sealant, making it impervious to oil, food and water, yet retaining a natural look.

Anti-bacterial products You may want to think twice before you buy one of the many 'anti-bacterial' products that have been launched for domestic kitchen use. The performance of such anti-bacterial washing-up liquids and impregnated chopping boards, dish cloths and bin liners – even sinks and worktops – varies widely in terms of killing bacteria, decontaminating surfaces or inhibiting bacterial growth. They may even do more harm than good according to some infection experts. Anti-bacterial products share a common factor with antibiotics in that they have the ability to kill all

bacteria, both good and bad. The most sensitive germs are initially destroyed, leaving behind the germs with some natural resistance, strains which have been termed 'superbugs' by some members of the medical world. With the beneficial bacteria gone, these 'superbugs' reproduce into bacteria that are virtually impervious to traditional treatment. Experts recommend using good old-fashioned bleach in the kitchen rather than newer anti-bacterial products. Other advice includes getting rid of washing-up bowls which can encourage cross-contamination of germs between chopping boards, plates and knives, and using disposable paper cloths instead of tea towels that could spread infection. Remember the 'peck of dirt' saying of our forefathers – we need good bacteria to fight the bad ones.

BELOW LEFT: Honed concrete worktops are a natural foil for the mix of petrol blue doors and dulled metal panels. A line of cooking oils and pots and pans adds colour to these bare surfaces. **BELOW CENTRE:** Hardwearing materials that transcend passing trends are often the most successful – like this uniform grid of white mosaic tiles – clean, efficient and timeless. **BELOW RIGHT:** Dark grey slate tiles form the backdrop for wall-hung brass taps and simple white pots crammed with utensils. The effect is simple, subtle and honest.

RIGHT: Long lengths of solid timber planks create a fluid and unified floor. Wood should always be sealed to protect from moisture. **BELOW LEFT:** Blue natural stone sourced from Belgium completes the natural palette of materials in this galley kitchen. **BELOW CENTRE:** Italian travertine floor tiles with a smooth, honed finish are both tough and slip-resistant. Surfaces can contain natural open pores that are normally filled with grout on installation or pre-filled at source. **BELOW RIGHT:** Painted white floorboards disguise any mismatched woods, blemishes and discrepancies as well as maintaining the freshness of this all-white decor.

FLOORING

A kitchen floor is primarily about comfort, durability and maintenance. Colour and design are of course important factors, but the type of surface material you choose needs to fulfil far more demanding practical requirements. A stone floor will last for generations and acquire the lovely patina of use and age, but it is much colder and noisier than a vinyl or linoleum, and is an unforgiving surface if you are on your feet all day long. Stone and tiled floors create crisp, functional surfaces but are hard on glass or china – breakages are more likely to occur, perhaps more frequently if you have small children. If you have an open-plan kitchen, you may want to define different zones by using contrasting floor materials or different floor heights. If the kitchen is a small area, however, you should use the same material to convey fluidity and unity.

Whichever type of flooring you choose, it is always better to get it laid by a professional who can advise on substrate, quantity required and any special finishes or treatments that will extend the life of the floor.

Material choices

Wood A timber floor is simple, versatile and naturally beautiful. There are many species to choose from, including creamy, variegated maple, reddish-brown cherry, oak and rich dark brown, almost purple-black, walnut. Softwoods such as pine are less expensive and a good choice if you are going to stain or paint the floors. (See page 129 for more information.) For a more decorative look, choose parquet flooring laid in blocks and panels.

Wood is a natural, living material so variations in batches and packs are a matter of course. Wood floors are also very sensitive to their surrounding climate, expanding in damp, humid conditions and shrinking when the air becomes dry. The boards therefore need to be acclimatised before they are fitted, at least 48 hours prior to installation. As such, seasonal cracking – small cracks between boards – is a common occurrence and should therefore be viewed as a characteristic of wood floors.

Timber floors should also be sealed to protect them from the damaging effects of water. Natural boards may come pre-sealed with a wax, oil or lacquer, but painted or stained floors should also be sealed.

A veneer of hardwood may be a good choice if you want the look of solid wood but haven't got the height space for joists. It is also less expensive than solid wood. A wood laminate floor is cheaper again.

Dirt and grit will act like sandpaper and destroy the protective surface of a wood floor, so vacuum, brush and mop regularly. Area rugs or mats can be used to protect high-traffic walkways and standing zones, such as in front of the sink and the fridge. Timbertec treatment leaves a wood floor neutral without varnish.

Tiles Glazed tiles and mosaics do not require any sealing or finishing, whereas unglazed versions need to be oiled and sealed when they are laid or else they will absorb water and stain easily. The finish will need redoing periodically to keep the floor in good condition. Encaustic tiles differ from ordinary tiles in that the pattern actually runs through the tile. The stoneware or clay is still in a semi-liquid state while the design is formed and produces a characteristic merging of colours.

Floor tiles are thicker than wall tiles so they will be harder to cut. Bear in mind also that tiling raises the floor level, so you will need to plane down the bottom of doors for extra clearance.

Porcelain tiles are denser and stronger than clay and available in larger slabs. They have a crisp, square edge that can be butted up tightly with minimum grouting to produce an almost seamless floor.

Terracotta tiles are also made from clay which is baked or fired. Terracotta retains heat and is therefore the warmest tile underfoot. Colours range from rich, dark and earthy terracotta to lighter shades of honey and ochre. Reclaimed and antique terracotta tiles have a leathery patina; they are usually moulded by hand, and some are even stamped with the maker's original monogram. Terracotta should be sealed

before and after grouting and finished with a wax polish. Regular waxing enhances the natural colour and provides protection against staining.

Paviors are another option. Non-slip and waterproof, they can be laid in a variety of patterns on a damp-proof base. They are also much more highly fired and need no finish.

Mosaic Built up from tiny tesserae of stone and marble, mosaics are used to create infinite designs, patterns and motifs. Special commissions are costly, however; instead you could simply use sheets of mosaics mounted on mesh for easy fixing and add simple borders to define edges. Mosaics need to be grouted for a finished appearance and cared for like tiles.

Stone Natural stone is tactile and enduring. Choose from limestone, slate, granite, sandstone, marble and travertine (a limestone/marble mix), depending on the colour and finish you want (see pages 135–136). A honed, matt finish will create an anti-slip surface while a riven stone like slate may have surface flaking, which should be brushed off before fixing.

Floor bases need to be clean, dry and free of grease and any loose debris. If the subfloor is not concrete, consult a qualified structural surveyor to make sure the floor can take the weight of the stone. Screeded or previously tiled floors are easiest to tile on to. Wooden floors require marine ply to be glued and screwed at 150mm intervals. All stone should be sealed, waxed or impregnated (depending on which type you choose) to prevent staining and acid erosion.

ABOVE LEFT: Farnsworth House by Mies van der Rohe. The rectilinear structure, divided by flat planes or service blocks, and widespread use of glass are complemented by travertine and marble. **ABOVE RIGHT:** Polished concrete floors add a sophisticated earthiness to this kitchen. **RIGHT:** The irregular surface veining of these green marble floor tiles gives an almost sea-like, watery effect to this Austrian kitchen. The inherent pattern is in stark contrast to the uniform lines of the cement worktop and graphic shapes of the appliances and furniture.

Concrete A utilitarian substance made up of cement powder, sand and water, concrete floors are affordable and inject a cool austerity into the kitchen. Slabs or tiles must be sealed against stains, and can be waxed or stained to give a more lustrous finish. Concrete can chip and crack.

Terrazzo A mix of glass or marble chippings and resin, terrazzo is hand-trowelled onto the floor and ground to a smooth, polished surface. It is smooth, tough, non-slip and available in any colour. Terrazzo must be laid onto a stable, non-moving surface such as concrete – an unstable surface may be prone to cracks. A hand-trowelled resin is preferable to a roller finish, which is much thinner and therefore prone to cracking. Terrazzo washes clean with hot, soapy water.

Linoleum 'Lino' has become a misnomer for cheap varieties of vinyl flooring, but is actually extremely durable, flexible, hygienic and easy to clean, as well as being warm and quiet underfoot. It is made in an environmentally responsible way from natural raw materials such as linseed oil, resin, wood-flour and chalk. The material is rolled into sheets and pressed onto a hessian backing (polyester for the tile format) then baked at high temperatures. Linoleum is resistant to acids, oils, fats and grease although spillages should be removed quickly. Marks left as a result of stubbing out cigarettes can easily be removed with gentle sandpapering. Linoleum comes with a factory finish to aid maintenance; spills, mud and dust can be quickly and easily wiped away. Colours range from neutral shades such as ivory and charcoal to vibrant colours like apple green and indigo, in plain and marbled finishes. Borders, square insets and feature panels can be added for a more dramatic look. Precision cutting technology means you can also create unique designs.

Vinyl This flooring is functional, comfortable and low-cost. A high-quality vinyl is thicker and made from 100 per cent PVC; cheaper versions contain fillers that make them more

brittle. Vinyl is ideal for kitchens, is available in an almost unrivalled range of colours, patterns, textures and designs, and can simulate virtually any type of hard flooring such as wood, stone and tiles. A hardwearing vinyl is waterproof, slip-resistant, mildew- and odour-resistant, and simple to keep clean (regular sweeping and mopping with a mild detergent is all that is needed). The subfloor needs to be clean, level, smooth and dry before the vinyl is laid. Another benefit is that vinyl is not thick like most natural flooring so there is no need to alter the heights of doors and skirting boards when it is installed.

Rubber A favourite with architects and interior designers, rubber is practical, hardwearing, warm, water-resistant, burn-resistant and quiet, the ideal material for use in the toughest environment. Rubber comes in a wonderful range of bold primaries and neutral tones, as well as different textures like studs and treadplates for extra grip underfoot. Some companies will also offer a colour-matching service.

Rubber tiles are easy to cut, so you can create unique patterns and designs. They are laid using an approved adhesive and expert installation is advised – once cut, the material cannot be repaired if the size is wrong. Alternatively, a 'poured' rubber floor will create an even tougher, seam-free surface. This must be carried out by an expert and given adequate time to 'set'.

To clean, simply mop with water or a gentle detergent, but remember, dirt may get trapped around the relief pattern of textured floors.

Cork A cork floor is warm, comfortable, lightweight and quiet underfoot. As well as natural hues, cork tiles are now available in a range of colours and with a tough PVC coating featuring photographic images such as leaves, pebbles and grass. Tiles are simple to install; basic DIY skills are all that is needed. Natural cork needs sealing to prevent wear and staining, but a PVC-coated version requires no special finishing, just cleaning with a damp mop and mild detergent. A hard wax finish creates an extra warm, anti-slip surface.

Carpet While carpet isn't generally recommended for use in the kitchen for practical reasons, coir or sisal matting, made from natural fibres such as coconut husks and agave plants, are far more resilient and hardwearing. Liquid spills can be prevented from soaking in immediately by pre-treating the flooring to create a protective, invisible shield around the fibres. Natural floor coverings will stain, however, so soak up the spillage promptly – dab the stain rather than rubbing it. For normal day-to-day cleaning, use a cylinder-type vacuum cleaner or the hard floor setting on an upright cleaner. Never use a steam cleaner.

Alternatively, hardwearing carpet tiles, made from polypropylene or nylon, are easy to cut and lay yourself. They have a special backing so underlay is not required, but prompt treatment is the most successful course of action for spillages. Carpet tiles, commonly associated with offices and public areas, have currently undergone a revival with new, ultra-modern designs such as urban pavement, denim and spots.

Metal Sheet metal or tiles in aluminium or steel will add a distinctive industrial edge to your kitchen, although they can be hard on tired feet. Non-slip 'tread plate' surfaces are the most practical. The tiles can be glued on to a flat wooden or concrete subfloor; if the floor is not level you should lay timber to flatten the surface first. Steel is harder than aluminium, although it will rust unless galvanised or powder coated. Aluminium tiles should not be grouted, as they are difficult to clean afterwards. Avoid leaving liquid on the surface for a long duration and re-polish when necessary using liquid polish and a soft cloth.

FAR LEFT: Metal tread plates are hardwearing, industrial and very practical. The change of floor materials from warm wood to cold metal is a bold demarcation of the different areas. **LEFT:** Bright blue rubber flooring is offset against this neon pink kitchen. Rubber tiles are good for kitchens used by children, being warm and extremely practical – and less harsh on the feet and knees than harder floors.

CABINETS

The style of kitchen furniture you choose will have a large impact on the look and feel of the room. If you opt for a fitted kitchen, the cupboards are permanently fixed and can be designed to fit the room's dimensions. There are three basic units: base cupboards that incorporate sinks, built-in appliances and storage (either a series of drawers; a cupboard; or a cupboard with one drawer above); tall units with room for shelves, pull-out larders or appliances; and wall cabinets which can have matching door fronts or glass panels for displaying crockery and glassware, for example. Some kitchens, especially smaller rooms, benefit from replacing wall units with open shelving. This will help to open up the space, relieving any feelings of claustrophobia – although it does call for extra tidiness. An unfitted or 'modular' style kitchen is based around moveable, freestanding units on legs that are designed to resemble pieces of furniture, such as a dresser or tallboy.

Budget kitchens generally offer less choice in terms of style and range of cupboard sizes, which may leave space-wasting gaps in your plan. However, more and more manufacturers are devising flexible approaches, allowing you to mix and match door fronts and create special features such as an angled breakfast bar or stepped island

unit. Remember that stock kitchen cupboards are less expensive and readily available. If you aren't keen on any of the door styles, consider buying off-the-peg carcases and commissioning doors from a carpenter. This way you can get the look you desire, yet still keep costs down.

Mid-range kitchens offer a broader choice of units, usually in 10cm increments with varying heights to make best use of space. Bespoke kitchens offer the ultimate in customisation – at a price. A tailormade kitchen isn't limited by any size or precedent, so you will get custom-made units to accommodate you and your kitchen requirements – whether it's a base cabinet with a special silverware drawer or a huge, robust chef's pantry. Wall cupboards can be built to the proportions of the room while difficult or small spaces can be utilised with 'specials' such as wine racks, spice drawers, tray slots or even window seats.

Behind closed doors

The quality of the material behind the door front is just as important as what you see on the outside. It's less a question of style and visibility than of stability and rigidity.

Kitchen carcases (the boxes behind the doors) vary in thickness depending on quality and price. A carcase that is made from 18mm-thick melamine-faced medium density fibreboard (MDF) is a good standard to aim for, and is more suitable than solid wood, which can warp or move. Carcases should have solid, rigid backs and fully adjustable legs that can take account of uneven floors and protect units from penetrating damp. Look out for coloured carcases that match the colour of your doors or pale grey versions that merge 'invisibly' into the background (as opposed to a gleamingly bright white), which will also suit the trend for steel and aluminium door fronts. Drawer boxes need to have solid sides, made of either wood or metal, with strong bases and smooth-action roller runners. The best drawers can glide shut with a push from your hip or foot, and close silently. The most expensive are made of wood with dovetailed

LEFT: Full-length frosted glass cupboards keep china and tableware free from dust, yet in sight, and work well with the glass skylight and door. **ABOVE:** A striking wall of flush-fitting units with rectangular recess utilises every inch of space and doubles up as a blackboard for leaving messages. The steel tubular extractor fan and black pendant light are dramatic but functional. **ABOVE RIGHT:** Lit above and below, this one-piece block of cupboards seems to float inches from the floor. Behind every door front lies hidden storage space or an appliance.

joints and waxed wooden runners. Full-extension drawers that extend the entire length of the drawer allow complete access to the contents, with everything immediately to hand. A kick-board or plinth can be installed to conceal the legs of base units or they can be left bare to become part of the kitchen design. This space can also be utilised in small kitchens for extra storage (shallow drawers can hold baking trays, frying pans or tea towels) or a plinth heater.

Cupboards are either framed or frameless. With a framed face, a rectangular frame outlines the carcase, strengthening it and providing a mount for the door to fit into. In-frame doors are better suited to more traditional, bespoke designs. A frameless door is cheaper to make. It fits flush with the carcase, is easy to hang and creates a simple, streamlined look. Metal hinges are stronger and more enduring than plastic and also allow for adjustment; clip-on versions allow greater flexibility as doors can be removed quickly and simply.

The doors

The choice of materials and finishes for kitchen doors has become increasingly sophisticated – from a tough rubber-coating to milky glass to ridged aluminium. At the same time, the style of the doors available is becoming much simpler and more streamlined to fit in with the increasingly popular straightforward, no-frills contemporary design. Before you choose your kitchen units, check that the door front is hardwearing and can withstand a variety of knocks and bangs from repeated opening and closing. It must also be easy to clean, especially if you have young children and animals when muddy paw prints and trails of sticky jam can become a daily occurrence.

Solid wood Use wood that has been kiln-dried or acclimatised over a period of months to the humidity of a kitchen, otherwise cupboards will warp or crack when installed. Slight seasonal cracking is to be expected.

FAR LEFT: A single cube of strong colour breaks up the band of uniform storage units. To minimise the glare from the reflective surfaces, the light source is concealed at the top and bottom of the wall units. **CENTRE LEFT:** Deep petrol blue units, chunky chrome handles and a chequerboard tiled flooring gives this kitchen a distinct 1930s feel. **ABOVE LEFT:** A wall of mirrors at the far end of this kitchen creates a space-enhancing illusion. The pale lime green units seem to continue endlessly. **BELOW LEFT:** Simple chrome shell grips on wooden door fronts are both timeless and good looking.

Hardwood doors can either be made from solid wood, which means they will be heavy and expensive, or a combination of solid frames and veneered centre panels. The panel provides extra stability and a more contemporary look, as the centre will be one piece of veneer rather than a number of flush planks.

Softwood is much cheaper but can lack an interesting grain, so doors are usually stained or painted. Cedar is popular for drawer linings because of its fresh, lingering aroma. Laminated bamboo is great for use as a kitchen door, it is very strong and resistant to knocks, and is unlikely to warp or swell as wooden doors can do in the humid conditions of a kitchen.

Veneers A veneer is a thin slice of wood, around 0.8mm, which is adhered to the front and back of a substrate of plywood, chipboard or MDF under high pressure. It can then be finished with two or three coats of two-part lacquer.

Since veneer is made by peeling thin layers of wood from a single log, cupboard doors have a sleek uniformity. They are also less expensive and more stable than solid wood but will create the same effect.

Laminates A high-pressure laminate is made from layers of coloured or patterned paper which are fused together under high pressure, finished with a tough melamine top layer and bonded to an MDF substrate. Laminates provide a tough, easy-to-clean surface and come in a wide range of colours and patterns including metallics and wood-effects. Make sure the front and back of the door is covered with laminate for strength and to prevent warping. Laminates should be cleaned with water and mild detergent. Persistent marks can be removed using a suitable cream cleaner, but harsh abrasives must not be used. Low-pressure laminate, known as melamine, is cheaper, thinner and less durable, and is more commonly used to cover carcases.

Lacquers Lacquered cupboards are usually at the top end of the price scale. They are available in a wide variety of colours – from pastel blue to scarlet to rich, chocolate brown – in a satin or high-gloss finish. The lacquer comes in two parts and is mixed prior to application and sprayed onto an MDF door. A number of coats are built up to give the door a tough, resilient finish.

Metals No longer the sole preserve of appliances and worktops, metals such as stainless steel, zinc and aluminium can bring a touch of industrial chic to kitchen cupboards and the result is strong and streamlined. Doors are rarely made from solid metal (which would be extremely costly); instead a thin metal skin (around 0.8mm) is wrapped around an MDF core, and given rounded profiles to eliminate sharp edges. Metals can be polished, matt, sandblasted, brushed or corrugated and extra decorative effects can be added with perforations, punch marks or by brushing. Polished stainless steel is clean and highly reflective but smears easily. Matt aluminium can be anodised and is a softer, whiter metal and looks good offset with thick, greenish glass; zinc ages to a nice patina while copper offers a warmer tinge. Some specialist metal companies can transform your existing kitchen by cladding doors and drawers in the metal of your choice. Many budget ranges also offer a stainless steel-effect laminate, which is much cheaper and easier to keep clean.

Glass Until now, glass was mainly used for centre panels in a kitchen door, as a means of decoration to break up a run of solid fronts and as a way to display crockery and glassware. Glass can be clear, sandblasted, frosted, ribbed or etched, depending on the look you require.

However, glass has recently come into its own and is now used to create complete kitchen doors, which are streamlined and easy to clean. Doors are made from 6mm-thick toughened glass with colour baked on to the back for extra durability. Instead of a handle, a neat circular cut-out will offer a streamlined look.

Paint Painted cabinetry allows you to choose literally any colour from the spectrum – from exuberant, vibrant shades to paler tones to pure white. Paint can also help create an earthy, lived-in ambience that you may not get with the more modern finishes. The classic, Georgian palette of neutrals – grey, olive and buttermilk – suits both traditional and contemporary kitchens while rich, strong colours like deep green, petrol blue and ox-blood red can add an injection of personality into an otherwise neutral look. You may decide to paint a single item, say a dresser or serving table in deep charcoal grey or bright azure to set off a predominantly timber kitchen. It is wise to experiment with different colours and sample pots before you go ahead – particularly with the bolder shades. Look for manufacturers who also offer a range of specialist decorative techniques including colourwashing, distressing and stippling. If you buy a handpainted kitchen from a bespoke manufacturer, it should be sealed with a coat of hardwearing lacquer. HPG is a rubber paint that gives a tough, durable finish, which is matt and velvet smooth to the touch.

You can also revamp old kitchen units yourself with a fresh lick of paint, but examine the original surface first. Melamine is smooth and non-porous, making it difficult to paint over – ordinary paints will flake and blister. Use a melamine primer as a base coat, then apply a melamine satin. All wood – either bare or painted – needs to be sanded and then primed. Sand to a smooth finish with sandpaper (don't use wire wool), remove the debris with a damp rag and apply a coat of primer. The primer penetrates the wood and grips the grain, providing a key for the next coat of paint. If you don't prime the wood, you'll get a patchy, uneven finish. MDF, the DIY-ers do-it-all material, must be primed first, otherwise the surface will soak up the paint like blotting paper. Always use formaldehyde-free MDF and wear a protective mask when working with it. Wooden doors can also be transformed with a coloured varnish. Rub down the surface with a fine abrasive paper and wipe down with white spirit, then apply varnish with a brush in even strokes along the grain of the wood.

ABOVE LEFT: Pale timber doors are matched by splashbacks made from identical panels turned on their side. The pair of pendant lamps continue the parallel lines running through the base units and splashbacks. ABOVE RIGHT: Interlocking blocks of wood and matt grey door fronts create a subtle pattern without the need for intricate design or bold colour. BELOW LEFT: A stainless steel tambour shutter can be pulled right down to the worktop to hide small appliances from sight, and keep them out of the reach of children. BELOW RIGHT: For a simple and modern interpretation of the 1950s kitchen, simply thread lengths of washable material on to a slim metal pole.

STORAGE

Storage is a fundamental part of a kitchen. There's simply no point in having a kitchen that looks fantastic if you have to bend, stretch and root around in the back of deep, dark cupboards to seek out your basic kit; not only will this be deeply irritating, it is also not energy-efficient. No matter how big the kitchen, you can never have enough storage.

Inadequate storage is usually less to do with lack of space and far more to do with careless design and bad organisation. So it is important from the outset to decide what you need to store, where you need to store it and how your kitchen will accommodate your needs. Fortunately, kitchen manufacturers have devised a host of clever behind-the-scenes storage solutions to make even the smallest kitchen an efficient, well-organised space. However, one of the great advantages of moving into a new kitchen is the opportunity to throw away all those things you never use and don't need and simply serve to clutter up your life – less is definitely more when it comes to a working kitchen.

FAR LEFT: Modular storage creates an organised feel. It is at its most effective when it ensures there is a place for everything from dried food, herbs and condiments to candles, plates and glasses. When not in use, two swing-open doors can be closed to shut away the kitchen. **LEFT:** Jams, preserves and bottles are neatly stored beneath the worktop. Handles are dispensed with, giving way to discreet cut-outs instead.

Show or conceal

The kitchen is a place that houses an incredible amount of diverse things – from dried foods to saucepans, washing powders to pet food, fresh fruit to rubbish bags. Deciding what is to be concealed behind cupboard doors and what is to be displayed on open shelves will affect the appearance of the room and also its practicality. Kitchen displays work best when they celebrate the beauty of everyday things. A bowl of lemons or a windowsill lined with homegrown herbs can be much more appetising than an artfully arranged collection of china.

Start with a few basic questions. Decide what you want on display: perhaps a row of wall-hung utensils near your cooking area or open shelving to keep herbs and spices? Or do you prefer a sleek, streamlined look with everything stashed out of sight? Visually speaking, this may suit an open-plan kitchen, part of a one-space loft apartment say, where an uncluttered look won't intrude on the rest of the space. However, fully fitted kitchens where absolutely everything is hidden behind cupboard doors can look too sterile and unlived-in. At the same time, over-cluttered kitchens can be muddling and tiring to work in.

The kitchen also contains areas where some of the most regularly used supplies and utensils need to be within easy reach. Only objects used every day, or at least once a week, deserve prime storage space – the areas within easy reach – usually somewhere between knee and eye level.

Decide what you need to be most accessible and arrange your kitchen accordingly. It's largely a matter of common sense – the equipment and utensils which relate to each area of activity should be stored or displayed close by. Logically, pots and pans should be stored near the cooker or hob with their lids off so that air can circulate, and in a position where dust won't collect inside. Try deep pull-out pan drawers with a separate pan lid rack or simply hang upside down from a hook by the handle.

Wicker baskets slotted in below the worktop keep vegetables fresh because they allow the air to circulate underneath. Keep herbs and spices and other essential foodstuffs close to the food preparation area, but remember that spices become unseasonably bland when stored too near heat. Store crockery in a plate rack over the sink or draining board where it can drip dry at the same time, or in cupboards near to the dishwasher to avoid carrying them to and fro.

Try not to keep things you use once a fortnight in a key space. Specialist appliances like ice-cream makers and yoghurt makers as well as large party platters can be in the less accessible storage areas, perhaps tucked away in the back of low cupboards, or if used really infrequently, perhaps even out of the kitchen altogether. Don't store bulky or heavy items, such as family-size bottles of fruit juice, too high up or too low down.

Small spaces

Finding room for all your pots, pans, plates, not to mention food, can be a problem in a small kitchen. Make good use of walls with ceiling-height units, interspersed with open shelving to help create a light, airy atmosphere. And exploit every inch of space with interior racking: full-extension,

BELOW LEFT: Vast lengths of chunky steel shelving marry utility with decorative display. This is a sturdy space, ideal for storing bulk supplies of kitchen essentials. **RIGHT:** This unique – and cheap – interpretation of the suspended ceiling rail means pans and utensils are easily accessible. **BELOW CENTRE:** Tailormade storage helps to promote a well-organised, visual feast for the kitchen. Tightly packed open shelving stands in contrast to the dangly loop of the shower-like tap and casually strung pots and pans. **BELOW RIGHT:** Uniform boxes of cubbyhole storage are good way of keeping tableware and accessories close to hand.

slimline units, corner carousels and even plinth drawers, which fit neatly under base units. A Magic Corner system is particularly useful and is designed to make full and easily accessible use of those dead spaces in a standard corner unit. Some kitchen manufacturers have also developed extra-deep base units with space at the back of the worktop for a range of accessories, including a pull-down chopping board and spice drawers – an ideal solution for narrow, single-line kitchens.

Larders and pantries

Larders and pantries need not be relegated to memories of a bygone childhood – both offer practical and cost-effective storage solutions, allowing you to see your food supplies at a glance.

The natural refrigeration of a larder is a time-honoured way of keeping a wide variety of foods fresh. Away from the heat of the kitchen but without the deep chill of the fridge, the larder allows certain foods like fruit and jams to mature and improve with age and keeps many others in good condition for considerable periods of time. The traditional location for a larder is on the north-facing side of the house, the side that never sees the sun, with as many external walls as possible, to take full advantage of the natural chilling and good ventilation.

Larders and pantries should be rodent-proof, cool, well lit, have easy-to-sweep floors and rows of sturdy shelves. Stone walls, a slate floor and shelves are perfect. The ambient temperature can be low enough to preserve vegetables and fruit, game, ham, sausages and salamis, jars of preserves, racks of wine and the odd leftover for overnight storage. The larder also makes an ideal location for bulk stores, which can then be decanted for everyday use in the kitchen.

However, many people today live in houses without larders or pantries and those with a basement find it is often too warm to use as a food storage room. In terms of space, a larder is a luxury for most home owners, although the same basic principle can be adapted to fit out a tall cupboard. Pantry cupboards can be ordered from bespoke kitchen companies, either as freestanding pieces of furniture or built-in with the rest of the kitchen. They are often double-doored, and open out to reveal shelves, wicker baskets, bread bins and wine racks.

If you do have the space, there is also an option of transforming an existing room or part of a room into a walk-in chilled food store. Popular in Scandinavia, air conditioning keeps the temperature of the larder-fridge at a regulated 5°C. The only limitation is that the temperature of the room where the warm side of the larder unit is placed cannot be lower than 4°C or higher than 26–27°C at all times.

Wine storage

Wine needs to be correctly stored if it is going to last. Few people have the space or the budget to create their own wine cellar, but if you do, it is best ventilated. All wine – red, white and rosé – should be stored lying on its side in a cool, dark place. In the kitchen, beware of storing wine too close to the oven, otherwise the variation in temperature will be too great. Simple wire or wooden racks can be adapted to fit most spaces and will carefully cradle your wine.

Wine enthusiasts will relish the prospect of a specially designed wine storage unit to house their wine collection. These units (which can fit under the worktop, much like a fridge) feature two temperature zones which can be set to serve wine at the exact temperature you want as well as set at 13°C (55°F) to duplicate the ideal storage temperature of cellars and caves.

FAR LEFT ABOVE: Narrow, pull-out racking utilises otherwise redundant space. The open, galleried sides allow easy access to the herbs, spices and bottles and keep them in place when the unit is opened and closed. **FAR LEFT BELOW:** A standard drawer is transformed into a terracotta bread crock keeping loaves fresh and moist. **LEFT:** Pale grey cubes of storage conceal everything from sight, even the dishwasher. The integral, lipped handles and large angled lamp maintain the utilitarian, almost office-like effect.

case study: KITCHEN STORAGE

Simplicity can be very difficult to achieve.
When Jan and Ann Hagelin commissioned
architect Nico Rensch to design the interior of
their loft, formerly a Victorian school, they
specified a pure white minimal look, with
extensive storage to hide all the clutter of everyday life.
The solution was to house all the working areas of the space,
from kitchen fittings and appliances to workstations, behind pristine
panels, technically a very demanding exercise in specialist joinery.

LEFT: The main working area
of the kitchen, where the
kitchen range, sink and boiler
are fitted, is screened by a pair
of bi-folding doors. **RIGHT:** View
looking down the loft space
from the kitchen counter to the
seating area at the far end. The
seating area is raised up on a
platform which itself contains
yet more storage space. The
bedroom is on the mezzanine
level, accessed by stairs
hidden behind dummy panels.
The space is heated underfloor.

ABOVE: Bi-folding doors under the mezzanine pull back to reveal a workstation. Fitting and constructing storage for such a seamless look is a very exacting task, particularly taking into account essential service runs for plumbing, underfloor heating and ventilation. The panels are made of MDF, spray-lacquered white, and close on press catches. A key consideration was to make the effect look just as elegant when the panels were open, which meant juggling with conflicting geometries. To the right of the workstation, another panel conceals the main entrance to the loft. **RIGHT:** The central island is made of MDF, with a formica top. An inset groove or 'shadow gap' makes the top appear to hover over the base and lessens the mass of the island. **FAR RIGHT:** Flooring throughout is a grey Spanish limestone, laid in large square slabs. Together with the all-white colour scheme, the overall result is a luminous, serene space that fully satisfies the clients' brief.

SCREENS AND DIVIDERS

Even though you may like the idea of an inclusive, open-plan kitchen, there will still be times when some form of screening or dividing may be invaluable. It could be a crescendo of whirring appliances or a permanent pile of dirty dishes that instigate such a screening – or simply perhaps a desire to shut oneself off from the rest of the household.

Whatever the reason, decide whether you want a flexible or permanent arrangement. Subdividing part of the kitchen into a utility room will immediately alleviate noise

levels. For chefs who prefer to keep their cooking and entertaining separate, hatches allow verbal contact with the guests, but keep meal preparation out of view.

A two-tiered island unit with a raised shelf or splashback is a practical way of shielding mess on the work side of the kitchen and instils a degree of privacy and concentration for the cook. These units gently separate, instead of brutally segregating the kitchen within an open-plan arrangement – the other half of the island becomes the perfect space for friends and diners to pull up a stool and chat to the chef

LEFT: A narrow galley kitchen is opened up by a simple serving hatch, which also ensures the kitchen feels less confined and means that the cook is not excluded from the rest of the room. **BELOW:** In an open-plan space, a two-tiered island unit with a raised shelf successfully hides the cook's handiwork from view. **RIGHT, ABOVE AND BELOW:** This is the ultimate hide-away kitchen. A vast multifunctional living space is cleverly divided up by the use of sliding screens. When the kitchen is screened off, it is still accessible through the ribbed glass door. The coloured screen distinguishes the living area from the kitchen space when the screens are closed.

A few steps and a sleek pane of glass subtly demarcate the kitchen from the rest of this space. Clutter can be hidden behind closed doors while minimal fittings and the pale colours enhance the airy, open-plan ambience. **ABOVE RIGHT:** A pivoting wood panel with a tiny, cut-out, circular finger pull becomes a modern-day serving hatch. **BELOW RIGHT:** The concrete worktop and lilac colour theme from the kitchen have been continued through to the next space to create a modern sideboard in the dining room. The only division is a subtle sandblasted glass panel.

without too much interference. A peninsula unit or breakfast bar is another visual demarcation and can be enhanced by continuing wall cupboards beyond the wall, and mounting them on 'legs' so that they sit above the worktop. Again, this adds an element of visual privacy yet maintains the fluidity of open-plan living at the same time. Moveable shelf or preparation units and bookcases can also hide kitchen mess and allow for more relaxed dining on the other side, while a food preparation unit on castors can be wheeled away when not in use.

To make maximum use of one-space living, site the kitchen along one wall and use sliding or folding panels to screen it off when not in use. Avoid side-hinged doors, unless you have adequate clearance around them for their outward swing. Use transparent materials like sandblasted glass and Perspex, which will screen the kitchen from sight, but nevertheless allow daylight to filter through at the same time. Alternatively, commission a builder or architect to create a completely 'fold-away' kitchen. The doors of the kitchen can be deep, full-height panels, lined on the kitchen side with shelves, and hung using large, very strong hinges to take the weight.

case study: KITCHEN DIVISION

In a converted Victorian industrial workplace, a kitchen
area takes centre stage, separated on one side from a dining
area by a bar counter and from the living area on the other by a
freestanding wall. When Dominic Richards bought the east London loft, the
upper level, with its high ceiling supported by exposed roof trusses, had already been
subdivided by a developer into a warren of small boxy rooms, including a galley kitchen.
Dominic, who likes to entertain, opened the space up again to allow the structural bones of the
architecture to show through and allow him to chat to his guests while cooking. A palette of
warm, earthy materials adds a robust sense of character. A wireless system has also been
installed so that a laptop can be used anywhere in the loft.

FAR LEFT: Looking from the dining area through to the kitchen. The floor is made of polished oak. Heating is supplied by a low-level coil radiator. **LEFT:** The free-standing wall that encloses the kitchen and separates it from the living area has a long horizontal slit cut into it, positioned just above the work surface to allow views through the space, as well as conversation between areas.

ABOVE: The refectory-style dining table is made of English oak, salvaged from a tree that was brought down during the storms of 1987, and set between two broad bands of limestone. A limestone-topped counter, dividing the kitchen from the dining area, provides an alternative eating area.

ABOVE RIGHT: The living area is furnished with generous sofas upholstered in nubbly wool. An integrated sound system allows music to be enjoyed in every area of the loft. The free-standing wall divides space without blocking internal views of the spectacular roof structure. **RIGHT:** The sleek kitchen is fitted with units faced in MDF. The worktops are made of limestone. The panel above the horizontal opening is Indian laurel wood. Concealed downlights in the underside of the units light the work surface.

Appliances have been steadily revolutionising the kitchen since the 1950s. We now have at our fingertips a host of labour-saving devices that have drastically cut down the time we spend preparing and cooking food as well as liberating us from some of the drudgery of daily chores. They have also become steadily more energy efficient and the latest advances in technology even communicate with us and keep us informed at every step. Whether it's to alert us that our cooking time is up or that our fridge door has been left open, these cutting-edge developments have the potential to change the way we live and how we use our kitchens, saving us time and energy like never before.

Fittings and

Appliances

Equally, fittings and appliances have become a focus of considerable design interest. Appliances, especially, have ditched their functional, white-box image to become must-have designer-label purchases, as aesthetically pleasing as the units and furniture that make up the rest of the kitchen. From huge stainless steel fridge-freezers to fingerprint-free aluminium washing machines and solid range cookers in rainbow bright colours – yellow, red, blue and green – their design is now almost as much of a selling point as their technology and efficiency.

But hi-tech wizardry and high-fashion can be quite a daunting prospect. Before you indulge in needless expense and complexity, ask yourself if an internet-linked fridge or neon pink light-up sink is really going to improve the quality of your life. Technology, when it makes life simpler, when it makes life easier, is an enormous advantage. Decide what range of functions you require, what level of sophistication suits you, and the merits of different sources of power. There are also questions of budget, maintenance, energy savings and performance to be considered, but remember, a kitchen is for the preparation of food and if you spend more time fiddling with technology and then cleaning that technology afterwards, you will actually have defeated the whole purpose of it.

This section sets out what is available in a rapidly changing market place so that you can make your own assessment as to whether an appliance is suitable for the kitchen you are planning, the cooking you are planning to do in it, and the money you need to invest to achieve it.

LEFT: Sleek ceramic hotplates set flush with a stainless steel worktop are as aesthetically pleasing as they are functional. This is a cookcentre that is not only streamlined and modern in appearance but also very easy to clean. **INSET LEFT:** Everyday kitchen gadgets should be reliable and long-lasting. Many have also become iconic designs. **RIGHT:** Hidden behind a matching fascia panel, a fully integrated dishwasher is a time-saving boon in today's kitchen. Storing plates and dishes nearby allows for easy transfer from the dishwasher.

Choose appliances that not only meet your practical needs, but also your kitchen style. A simple four-burner gas hob and an 'invisible' extractor fan create a neat, unobtrusive cooking area in this incredibly simple, all-white kitchen.

COOKERS, OVENS AND HOBS

When it comes to the kitchen's primary function – cooking – you want a high-quality, brand-name appliance. This way you can be assured of a sound investment with reliable performance. If you know what brand you want, many leading appliance manufacturers employ home economists who will give free cooking demonstrations at their head showrooms. If you're undecided about a specific brand or model, then head for the high street where many kitchen showrooms have a wide range of working machines and can arrange demonstration days to show the benefits of each appliance.

Cookers

An all-in-one freestanding cooker with four electric hotplates or gas burners on top, and one or two ovens below, is still the most cost-effective cooking appliance on the market. This type of cooker can stand alone or slot in between two base cupboards and is easy and cheap to install. (For a separate built-in oven and hob you may have to rip out your kitchen and start from scratch.) Moreover, you can easily upgrade your freestanding cooker as most come in a standard 60cm width, and will slot smoothly into the space of your old model. If you have limited space, try a smaller 50cm-wide cooker or even a mini table-top version with two rings and an oven.

There is now a much wider selection of these 'entry-level' cookers on the market, with hi-tech features and sleek metal finishes to rival the built-in machines – multifunction fan ovens, wok burners, dual fuel models (electric oven, gas hob) and plenty of safety features. Grills are usually set inside the oven, which does restrict your ability to roast and grill at the same time; a separate grill cavity or double oven is a more flexible solution.

Range cookers

The craze for range cookers has been partly fuelled by cookery programmes on TV, which have linked them to the world of high-profile professional cooks, but also by the huge diversity of range cookers that are now available. Whether it's industrial stainless steel or the traditional, farmhouse Aga, range cookers now form the centrepiece of many kitchens, whether traditional or modern.

Enamelled, cast-iron ranges like Agas and Rayburns run off natural or bottled LP (liquefied petroleum) gas, oil, electricity or solid fuel. They release heat through the ovens and hotplates in a consistent way, without the need for a direct heat source. This radiant heat preserves all the flavour, moisture and texture of food. There are generally two ovens without temperature controls; the hot oven is for roasting, the cool one for slow cooking. Four-oven Agas also have a baking oven and warming oven. The two hotplates, one for boiling and one for simmering, are also ready to use at any time. The insulated covers keep heat in when the hotplates are not in use and are useful for drying and airing laundry. In addition, some ranges can also provide you with central heating and hot water. Cast-iron ranges must be installed on a solid, level floor, which can take the weight of the appliance, usually around 300kg.

Manufacturers of professional catering equipment have introduced domestic range cookers so we can emulate restaurant chefs in our homes. These robust and powerful cookers are more controllable than the traditional Agas and often provide up to six burners, with a fish-kettle, wok burner and griddle plate to accommodate the most inventive cooking. Two large-capacity ovens, a separate grill and warm storage drawer (for proving bread, warming plates or light storage) complete what is the ultimate cookcentre for the serious chef.

Such quality does not come cheap, however. Balance their good looks and high performance against how much you will use a range cooker and what you cook. Remember also that you'll need a lot more space. Measuring from 90cm to 150cm wide, they are often deeper than the standard 60cm oven. Unless they are used as freestanding pieces, ranges often require made-to-measure cupboards, and are more easily accommodated in a bespoke kitchen than a standard one.

If, however, you still hanker after a range but don't have the available space or budget, choose a range-style cooker. These vary between 55cm and 70cm wide with one or two ovens and four hotplates. Although not as powerful or imposing as the real thing, these mini ranges are available in virtually all the colours and trimmings as their big brothers.

Built-in cooking

Choosing a separate built-in oven and hob is usually more expensive, but offers greater flexibility for design and practicality. Ovens can be built in under the worktop or at eye level in a wall cupboard for easy grilling and less bending and lifting. You can also personalise your cooking kit by mixing fuel types. A gas hob and electric oven is still the most popular combination; however, a row of two-burner domino hobs (as opposed to a standard four-burner hob) allows you to customise your hob cooking by installing two gas burners and two ceramic hotplates side by side, in addition to other specialist features like a wok ring or barbecue grill.

Ovens

When choosing ovens, try not to be intimidated by industry jargon and hi-tech features. Do your meals consist of one-pot cooking or a combination of methods? For how many do you cook and what sort of food? Only you know what you cook, and therefore what type of oven will suit you.

Electric There are three types of electric ovens: conventional, fan oven or multifunction. The basic electric oven with conventional top and bottom heat produces a graded temperature, which is hottest at the top, so the centre is the best place to cook your food.

A fan oven draws air in from the oven via a powerful fan, then heats it up and forces it back into the oven cavity. By continuously circulating hot air around the oven, the desired temperature is achieved much more quickly, saving both time and energy, as little or no pre-heating is required. Heat penetrates food faster and more uniformly, and there are

LEFT: A French range with double oven and gas hob offers plenty of cooking capacity and flexibility. The cream enamelled doors and brass trim suit the simple, Shaker-style kitchen units. **INSET LEFT:** The Aga is a classic, time-honoured cooking fixture that gets better with age. The two ovens and two hotplates are kept constantly heated – ready to use at any time. **ABOVE:** Robust and powerful, a cooking range can dominate the kitchen – this is an appliance for the serious cook. The vast extraction pipe keeps the kitchen odour-free.

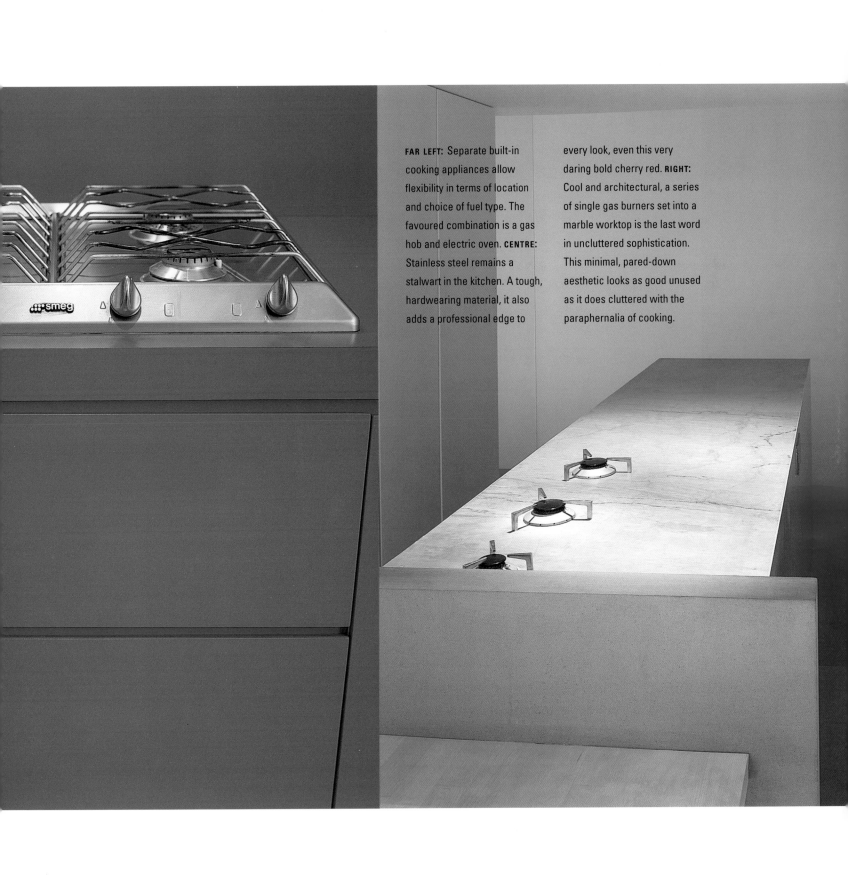

FAR LEFT: Separate built-in cooking appliances allow flexibility in terms of location and choice of fuel type. The favoured combination is a gas hob and electric oven. **CENTRE:** Stainless steel remains a stalwart in the kitchen. A tough, hardwearing material, it also adds a professional edge to every look, even this very daring bold cherry red. **RIGHT:** Cool and architectural, a series of single gas burners set into a marble worktop is the last word in uncluttered sophistication. This minimal, pared-down aesthetic looks as good unused as it does cluttered with the paraphernalia of cooking.

also no cold spots in the cavity, making this oven perfect for batch baking. Fan ovens are fast and economical, but can sometimes be noisy.

Multifunction ovens combine the two cooking methods to give you a really comprehensive appliance. They can include up to 10 different cooking functions including 'hot air grilling' for a rotisserie effect without the need for turning, and 'defrost' which circulates unheated air throughout the oven to cut defrosting times, ideal for delicate items like cream-based gateaux. Other functions allow you to steam, cook pizzas to perfection (crisp base and moist, melting topping) and bake bread. Some top-of-the-range ovens even include a list of pre-programmed recipes. You enter your chosen programme (say, leg of lamb cooked from frozen to medium rare), add the weight and the oven takes care of the rest. It will switch off automatically and finish cooking the dish using residual heat. You can even store your own recipes in the memory. Again, you need to weigh the cost of such an appliance against how useful these features are.

Gas Many top chefs still prefer a gas oven as it creates a moist atmosphere, keeps food tender and prevents overcooking. It is also perhaps more controllable. Gas ovens create a zoned heat with the centre of the oven heating up to the selected gas mark, and the top half hotter and the bottom cooler. Fanned gas systems are also available, offering even temperatures throughout the oven, which save energy by reducing heating up and cooking times.

Cleaning Pyrolytic self-cleaning ovens heat up to 500°C burning any deposits of grime and grease off the walls to leave a fine ash, which is easily wiped away. This takes around 2–3 hours and can be programmed to run overnight using off-peak electricity. For safety reasons, the oven door

locks automatically when cleaning. Catalytic oven liners are covered with a special coating which absorbs grease like blotting paper, until high temperatures during cooking destroy it. These clean only the areas of the interior where they are fitted and you will have to replace the linings periodically. Otherwise look out for smooth, non-porous enamel surfaces that are easy to wipe clean.

Capacity Don't forget to check the cooking capacity of the oven. A standard 60cm-wide single oven has around 55 litres of useable space. This will give you two or three

ABOVE: A row of narrow domino hobs creates a personalised cooking zone. Here, a deep-fat fryer, gas burners and a griddle plate are installed side by side to cater for every culinary whim. **RIGHT:** A range cooker 'look' is achieved by building in an extra-wide single oven and hob. With a matching stainless steel trim, splashback and hood, these appliances look very well integrated.

ABOVE: A black ceramic glass hob is offset with a steel trim and matching single oven. Some electric ovens, such as induction ovens, are almost as controllable as their gas counterparts. **BELOW LEFT:** Chunky control knobs, robust cast-iron pan rests and gleaming cookware are the ingredients of a modern-day cookcentre. **BELOW RIGHT:** A freestanding range with two ovens offers greater cooking flexibility for large families. The simple lines of the stainless steel bar handles are echoed on the kitchen door fronts.

cooking shelves at any given time or space for a 14kg turkey (the average-sized, family turkey is around 6–7kg). Double ovens are more convenient and flexible, and feature a smaller second oven with grill, with around 30 litres of space. A full-sized double oven measures 90cm high and can only be built-in at eye level. If you are hindered by lack of space, a built-under double oven measures 72cm high and fits neatly under the worktop. Wider single ovens (either 70cm or 90cm wide) are also more versatile and offer up to 30 per cent more cooking space than standard.

Safety If you have small children, don't forget to ask about low-temperature double- or triple-glazed doors. Even when the interior reaches 200°C, the surface stays at around 50°C. A child-safety control will lock all oven functions, while a safety cut-out device switches off the heat after a certain time. Eye-level ovens also remain out of the reach of small, inquisitive children.

Hobs

Manufacturers have been dreaming up a different type of hob for every conceivable cooking method. Domino hobs are by far the most flexible. These modular, two-plate hobs can be assembled in any configuration in order to meet your culinary requirements. Choose from a two-ring gas burner, two-plate ceramic hob, barbecue grill, wok ring, steamer and even a deep-fat fryer. These hobs can be built in separately or in combination with each other using connecting surfaces. Some hobs even flip up and down independently, allowing you to choose which domino you want to cook with, then flip the others up to free the extra worktop space underneath.

Gas This is still the most popular choice for hobs because it is instant and highly controllable. Most hobs include a simmer burner (around 1kW), a high-speed burner (around 2.6kW) and two standard burners (around 1.7kW). A larger five-burner hob is even more versatile and usually includes a powerful double- or triple-ringed wok burner (around

3.5kW or 4kW) or a central fish-kettle burner. One useful safety feature to consider is a flame failure device – if the flame is accidentally extinguished, by a draught, for example, then the gas supply automatically cuts off.

Electric The most basic electric hob is the sealed-plate version, but these are slow to heat up and cool down. Ceramic glass hobs provide a smooth, streamlined surface, set flush with the worktop, which means that you can simply wipe it clean. Halogen rings heat up faster than radiant rings but cannot match gas for speed and control. Induction hobs are the nearest you'll get to gas standards in terms of controllability and responsiveness, but they don't come cheap. Unlike standard ceramic hobs, heat is transferred directly to the bottom of the pan (and hence the contents of the pan) and wastes no energy heating the cooking zone or the hob. Only certain pans work with an induction hob, namely anything that a magnet would stick to such as cast iron and enamelled steel. If you want to experiment with gas and electric cooking, you could try a dual fuel hob which features two gas burners and two ceramic or halogen rings.

Tepan units are ideal for cooking healthy stir fries. The large circular stainless steel hotplate is set into a work surface, and when heated, forms a shallow dip in the middle so no liquid can escape. There is also a mobile version which can be wheeled out into the garden for an exotic alternative to the barbecue.

Extractor fans

There's nothing worse than a kitchen filled with strong cooking odours and greasy steam, especially in open-plan spaces, so investing in proper extraction is crucial. There are two types of extractor fans: ducted (extractor) or recirculating. Extractor fans are the most effective system, and take grease, steam and smells outside the house via ducting. It is best to site your extractor near to an outside wall for optimum efficiency – manufacturers recommend a maximum ducting length of 5m on a straight run, deducting

1.2m for every 90-degree bend. If, however, you live in a block of flats without an accessible external wall you will need a recirculation model. Stale air is drawn in and purified using grease and charcoal filters, before re-entering the kitchen. Most fans can be adapted for both extraction and recirculation systems. Position the hood carefully above your hob: too close and the steam may escape around the sides; too far away and the steam may disperse before it reaches it. For gas hobs, the minimum distance is around 65cm; for electric reduce this to 50–55cm.

Power levels Too much power is unnecessary. Before choosing a hood for your kitchen work out the volume of the room to be ventilated by multiplying length x width x height. A good ventilation system will change the air in a room 10 times per hour, so multiply this figure by 10, to give the minimum extraction rate required for your kitchen. Remember to ask about noise levels, particularly important in an open-plan setting. Aim for around 55–60 decibels as a benchmark.

There are many designs available, from brushed steel and glass canopy hoods to built-in telescopic hoods that fit between two overhead cupboards and slide out when in use. Some come with a run-on feature that will continue ventilating for 10 minutes after you finish cooking.

Microwaves

These appliances have become almost universal in the home, but their use tends to be limited to reheating pre-cooked food and microwave dinners. Many users are

BELOW LEFT: This glass and stainless steel extraction fan is crucial for eliminating unwanted cooking odours, steam and grease, but also adds a sculptural centrepiece to this kitchen. **BELOW CENTRE:** A built-in extractor fan whirrs into action when the matching front panel is pulled out – simple, unobtrusive but, most importantly, effective. **BELOW RIGHT:** The glass canopy of this circular extractor fan is continued along the length of the worktop to provide useful extra shelf space for storing equipment. Metal U-shaped bars are used for hanging utensils while cooking. **RIGHT:** A custom-made extraction unit not only takes away cooking smells and steam, it is also fitted with recessed spotlights for focused task lighting along the island.

unaware of the versatility and real benefits of microwave cooking, which can help retain vitamins, minerals and colour in our foods that can be lost in boiling, for example.

Microwaves use electromagnetic waves to heat food. When they strike the cooking food, the microwaves cause the water molecules within to vibrate at great speed. In turn, friction between these vibrating molecules generates the heat that cooks the food. The heat therefore originates within the food rather than outside it as in a conventional oven or hob. Because the vibrating continues after the microwave is switched off, you need to allow standing time when the cooking process is completed. Some machines with a steam button and specially designed 'steamer' accessory, allow you to steam cook rice, vegetables and fish in your microwave. The water in the base of the steamer reaches boiling point and is then maintained at a simmer throughout the cooking time.

The combination microwave oven integrates fan cooking or a grill with the benefits of a microwave. It will produce food that looks traditionally cooked (browned, roasted or crisped) but in about half the time and energy consumption of conventional cooking. These combination machines are particularly useful as they can double up as a traditional oven, should you need extra oven space. If you want to build in a combination microwave with your single oven,

make sure it is installed at a comfortable height so you can reach over the drop-down door (side-opening doors are for standard microwaves). It may be a good idea to build it in below the single oven or on its own below the worktop.

Power, performance and capacity vary according to manufacturer and model; full-size models usually have a 30–40 litre capacity, although compact microwaves are great for small kitchens. The important thing to look for here is the diameter of the glass turntable (can you fit in awkward-sized dishes?). Otherwise, a 'stirrer' system (usually found on combi-ovens) eliminates the need for a turntable.

Some models also come with automatic cooking and defrosting programmes and a memory so you can store the cooking times of your favourite recipes. A talking microwave has also been developed to meet the needs of the elderly and visually impaired.

If you want your microwave built into base or wall cupboards, buy one with proper ventilation that is specifically designed for such installation. An existing microwave can be adapted with special vents and baffles but this kind of customisation is costly. Otherwise freestanding models can sit happily on a worktop or shelving unit and come in a wide range of colours and finishes to suit – cool metals like stainless steel and brushed aluminium, white, bold colours and even ultra-modern, semi-transparent designs.

Steam ovens

Steam cooking is a quick and easy way to cook and eat healthily as it retains minerals, vitamins and moisture better than any other cooking method. Steam ovens work in various different ways, but instead of boiling or immersing food in water, they surround and cook it with steam (a visible white mist containing small water droplets), thus preserving the natural goodness.

The latest generation of built-in steam ovens are sleek, hi-tech reinventions of the bulky table-top pressure cooker. There are two types of steam oven – those that cook with pressure and those that cook without. A pressurised system is said to cut cooking times by up to 50 per cent using temperatures of up to 120°C (good for cooking solid foods like potatoes). Steam is created in a generator outside the airtight food chamber and forced back in, pressure cooking foods very quickly.

Pressure-less steam cooks food under normal atmospheric pressure. It is not as aggressive as a pressure cooker and the food's consistency and natural appearance survive largely unscathed.

Some steam ovens are plumbed into the water supply, and after cooking, any residual water automatically drains out the back of the appliance or can be saved for making stock. Other systems do not require any drainage or fixed water connection, and instead use removable water reservoirs which are filled manually with cold water.

If you haven't got space for a steam oven, some multifunction ovens feature a steam facility. The steam can be used on its own or in conjunction with other cooking modes (usually fanned or base heat) to create a moist and humid atmosphere that gently seals and enhances the food's natural moisture. A joint of meat thus remains succulent inside with a crisp, brown skin on the outside.

FAR LEFT: Built in at a more comfortable eye level, this combination microwave mimics the benefits of a traditional oven, such as grilling and browning, but in a fraction of the time. **LEFT:** Microwave ovens are frequently used for reheating ready-made meals and are often underrated for their ability to cook foods nutritiously. A built-in model should also include suitable ventilation. **ABOVE LEFT:** A built-in steam oven is a luxurious addition to the kitchen's repertoire of appliances – but it can be costly. **ABOVE RIGHT:** Steam cooking helps retain minerals, vitamins and moisture in our food, and can make a contribution to healthy eating.

FRIDGES AND FREEZERS

Refrigeration has perhaps had a greater impact on our cooking, eating and shopping habits than almost any technological development. Choose a fridge and freezer based on the size (and potential size) of your family; your work, shopping and cooking habits; the size and style of your kitchen; and of course on your budget.

Fridges vary from a huge American-style, side-by-side fridge-freezer with capacious and versatile storage space and a built-in crushed ice and water dispenser to unobtrusive built-in appliances with matching kitchen door fronts that fit neatly beneath the worktop. Remember to look at how the space is organised inside your fridge as well as the gross interior volume. Features like height-adjustable shelving, including split-width shelves to accommodate tall bottles, add flexibility and should ideally be made from easy-to-clean, toughened glass. Doors should also offer good storage with removable shelves, extra-deep balconies (holding up to 5-litre containers) and covered dairy compartments. In the freezer, non-tip drawers with solid drawer fronts will keep temperature loss to a minimum.

FAR LEFT: Reminiscent of a 1950s American diner, the bold colour and curved lines of this fridge have now reached an almost iconic status. **INSET LEFT:** Modern fridge-freezers can be used to make a strong statement in the kitchen.
ABOVE: Creating an assortment of storage cupboards on this odd-shaped wall influenced this Mondrian-esque design. A jigsaw of orange and turquoise door fronts (which hide a tall fridge and cupboard space) are interjected with the glint of stainless steel ovens.

Not all food should be stored in the fridge at exactly the same temperature – dairy produce, meat, fresh fruit and vegetables all have their own optimum storage conditions. That's why some refrigerators feature multi-zone cooling, controlling the temperature and humidity of specific areas so that different foods are chilled to exactly the right temperature. For instance, humidity-controlled salad drawers help food stay crisper while a 0 degree chiller compartment means perishable goods such as meat and cheese last twice as long. Indicator lights and temperature guides reassure you that food is being safely stored.

As well as conventional upright models, there are also hi-tech fridge and freezer 'drawers' that pull out much like a chest of drawers. These designs are perfect for providing extra refrigeration, especially when built in under an island unit, or for smaller studio apartments where space may be at a premium.

RIGHT: This gleaming hi-tech American-style fridge-freezer incorporates a cold-water and ice dispenser built in to one of the doors. CENTRE RIGHT: An expansive, stainless steel fridge-freezer is a classic addition to this predominantly all-white kitchen. FAR RIGHT: Huge American-style refrigeration units often have the fridge and freezer standing side by side, and can store an enormous amount of food.

Technology

Frost-free freezers circulate a stream of cold air through the freezer cavity, freezing food swiftly and preventing ice from building up on shelves and walls. They also prevent food sticking together and help maintain texture and flavour. Your freezer should carry at least a three-star rating (-18° C), so you can store pre-frozen food for up to three months.

Intelligent cooling maintains an even temperature control throughout the fridge and will temporarily direct cool air to warmer areas, if say the door is left open. In fridge-freezer units, look out for dual compressors with two motors that allow you to control the fridge and freezer separately.

Internet-linked fridges look set to transform the kitchen into the true technological nerve centre of the home. These multi-media appliances have TV, radio and internet access from a built-in, touch-screen LCD. It means that while you cook, you can re-stock your food supplies on-line, look up new recipe ideas and email friends and relatives without having to leave the kitchen. The fridge can also check itself routinely and if a problem occurs, send an alarm call direct to the service centre. In time, it is also likely to tell you what foods have reached their sell-by date and order more for you at the same time!

What do you need?

The refrigerator is an important piece of kitchen equipment so you should ask yourself these key questions before you make a decision:

▸ How often do you shop for fresh food? Do you need more fridge space than freezer space?

▸ Do you want a fridge with a freezer compartment? If you already have a separate freezer, you probably want a larder fridge instead.

▸ Do you want a freestanding appliance or a built-in version? Integrated models can be disguised with panels that match kitchen units whereas freestanding fridges are available in almost every colour and finish possible – from bold red to pastel blue to sleek aluminium.

▸ If you choose a built-in model, is eye-level height more convenient than under the worktop?

Energy labelling

Refrigeration is becoming increasingly energy-efficient. By law, manufacturers must disclose the energy efficiency of their appliances. Energy labels have existed since 1995 and show how efficient a fridge or freezer is by using a letter rating from A–G. A is the most efficient and signifies low running costs and maximum care for the environment while G is the least efficient. An A-rated fridge is said to cost half as much to run on a yearly basis than an equivalent C-rated appliance. No new fridge or fridge-freezer should contain CFCs (chlorofluorocarbons) and HFCs (hydrofluorocarbons) which have been linked to the 'greenhouse effect'. However, your old fridge may contain them, so dispose wisely – there may also be controls on disposal – your local authority should be able to advise you.

DISHWASHERS

When choosing a dishwasher, don't opt for complicated machines with excess gadgets. Be conscious of energy, water and detergent consumption. At the end of the day what you want is efficiently cleaned and dried dishes. Having said that, dishwashers are deemed to be more cost-effective than washing by hand and it is estimated that we can spend around 300 hours every year washing up at the sink. Top-of-the-range dishwashers use approximately 14 litres of water compared to 40 litres for handwashing a similar load. Not only that, dishwashers are more hygienic and can wash at higher temperatures (up to 70°C) than your hands can tolerate.

Features

Modern dishwashers are very efficient and use surprisingly little water and energy to wash a full load, mainly as a result of sensors or 'fuzzy logic' systems that allow the machine to 'think for itself'. The sensors analyse the degree of soiling in the wash water and calculate the best programme and temperature to do the dishes as economically and effectively as possible. There is a vast and bewildering range of programmes and special features on offer. Intensive, Normal and Eco programmes are probably the most widely used although a Quick Wash is handy for small loads and a 40°C programme is good for delicate glasses and china.

Machines with two revolving spray arms, fitted top and bottom, wash best, while efficient filter systems remove food and debris from the wash water. Useful features to look out for include flexible interior features such as height-adjustable top baskets that can take large plates and fold-down plate racks which create space for casserole dishes and large saucepans. It's also a good idea to consider a machine with an anti-flood system that switches off the water supply in the event of a leak.

Stainless steel interiors are more durable and less likely to take on odours or stain than enamel. However, some metals, such as copper and silver, may discolour because of a reaction to the steel.

ABOVE: Dishwashers ease the aftermath of dinner parties and gatherings, and the range of styles and matching door fronts mean that they will merge in with your kitchen units.

Energy and noise

Energy labels allow you to work out the energy and water costs (if you are water-metered) for a wash cycle. The label shows efficiency, cleaning and drying performance, rated A to G, with A being the best. Triple-A-rated dishwashers are becoming more widely available.

Make sure the operating noise is a barely audible hum. Sound is measured in decibels and the average dishwasher emits around 45–49dB. Look for something around 42dB – which is quieter than a boiling kettle – to help maintain a peaceful, relaxing environment.

Size

Dishwashers come in two main sizes: a full-size 60cm or slimline 45cm. The full-size models take approximately 12 place settings and slimline models around eight (one place setting equals ten pieces of crockery and cutlery). There are also compact, countertop versions which are said to be able to handle washing up for a party of five.

Choose a freestanding dishwasher if you want the unfitted look. A fully integrated model will be completely concealed behind a full-length kitchen door with the control panels hidden on the inside top rim of the door. Semi-integrated units have the control panels on show.

LAUNDRY

If you have the space, a separate washing machine and tumble dryer will give you the most flexibility, allowing you to dry one full load while washing another.

Washing machines

The average machine uses 60 per cent of the water and 40 per cent of the electricity that it would have needed 10 years ago. This is down to fuzzy logic technology, a computer chip that monitors every procedure and basically 'thinks' for you. For each load, it senses the correct wash time, decides which way to wash and uses the precise amount of water for the best results. It can even detect any excess detergent and add more water should it need to. This way, the amount of water and electricity required are always at a minimum. Most washing machines take a 5kg load but some models have a 7kg drum capacity, handy for larger families and can save time, money and effort. Bigger porthole doors which open at a 180-degree angle flat against the machine are easier for loading and unloading your washing.

Recent innovations include a washing machine which features two drums rotating in the opposite directions at once. It is designed to replicate handwashing after research showed that 15 minutes of handwashing got clothes cleaner than 67 minutes in the best washing machine. Another design has introduced a removable wash tub. The idea is that you can colour code your dirty clothes with different-coloured plastic tubs (i.e. green tub for whites, blue for coloureds); then your chosen laundry basket can be placed straight into the machine. When the wash is finished the tub is removed and the entire load taken straight to the washing line or tumble dryer. It is supposed to ease loading and unloading and prevent the risk of rogue socks staying in the drum and potentially infiltrating the whites wash.

Aim for a machine with an A energy efficiency rating to cut electricity usage and an A wash performance to tackle the worst and most stubborn stains. Triple-A-rated machines also offer excellent spin efficiency, guaranteeing a dryer fabric for reduced drying time. If you use a tumble dryer,

choosing a washing machine with an A-rated spin, instead of one with a G-rated spin will halve your tumble-drying costs. Spin speeds can range from a gentle 400 rpm up to a vigorous 1,600 rpm. As far as programmes are concerned, a low-temperature Hand Wash programme is useful for any clothes with a handwash label while Short Wash can reduce the length of a main wash programme by around 50 minutes. To take advantage of the lower electricity tariffs at night, delay time features allow you to programme the machine to start up to 19 hours later.

You also need to decide between a front and top loader. Top loaders take up less space and some people find them kinder on the back, as you don't have to bend down so far. There are also shallower 34cm- and 40cm-deep models available (a standard washing machine is 60cm deep) which are great for a small kitchen, utility room or older kitchens where narrower work surfaces can't always accommodate regular-sized appliances.

Tumble dryers

Tumble dryers are available as traditional vented machines or condenser models. Vented dryers are cheap and fast. Hot damp air is vented from the machine to the outside via a hose, so it needs to be sited on an external wall, which can restrict room planning. A condenser system is slower but the appliance can be fitted anywhere. These dryers use a heat exchanger to convert hot air to water, which is then collected in a special reservoir. Some models even have an indicator to remind you when the container needs emptying.

Washer-dryers

Combined washer-dryers are good if space is limited, although they can only dry half the washload at a time. Overloading the machine in the drying mode will prevent the contents from drying properly, cause creases and may even lead to a breakdown.

Assess noise levels before you buy. Special insulating panels around the machine cabinet and base can be installed to reduce noise. Built-in machines are also quieter.

SMALL APPLIANCES AND BASIC EQUIPMENT

As well as large appliances, kitchens are also home to numerous smaller pieces of equipment and gadgets. Many of these have been the focus of immense design interest, and shops are filled with rows of gleaming saucepans, retro-style toasters, sleek, cordless kettles, chrome blenders and funky bottle openers.

It is not uncommon, however, for a lot of tools and gadgets to end up buried and forgotten at the back of cupboards, taking up valuable storage space. As a sensible rule of thumb, any item in your kitchen should be able to justify the burning questions 'What does it do?' and 'How often do I use it?' Frequently used items should be within easy reach of where they are most needed, preferably on the worktop, while rarely used machines are best stored in out-of-reach cupboards and drawers. An appliance garage (a worktop-mounted cupboard with a pull-down tambour or roller shutter) is great for stowing less attractive, small appliances out of sight.

Basic kit

Basic kitchen utensils perform specific tasks, functions that will take much more time and effort with improvised equipment. You don't need a great many of these tools, but the following are indispensable in any kitchen: a lemon squeezer, sieve, funnel, colander, carving fork, can opener, corkscrew, potato peeler, potato masher, apple corer, balloon whisk, ladle, basting spoon, spatula, wooden spoon, rolling pin, pastry brush (avoid one with nylon bristles), cheese grater, salt bowl, pepper mill, kettle and a large, sturdy chopping board (the best are made from end-grain maple). All of these perform very specific tasks that are difficult to improvise and will certainly take you longer and require a great deal more effort if you don't have the right tool to hand. A pair of sharp kitchen scissors will serve as both poultry shearers and herb snippers, and can also be used to trim fat or the stems of cut flowers, clip recipes, cut through packaging and other general duties.

A good set of well-made chefs' knives is vital and will make food preparation as effortless as possible. You will need three – in 8cm, 12cm and 20cm sizes, together with some skewers, a carving knife, a palette knife and a bread knife with a serrated edge. Carbon steel blades last the longest but will need to be carefully dried and cared for to prevent rusting. Stainless steel blades will not corrode but are harder to sharpen. Store your knives safely in a block, rack or magnetic holder that can be attached to a wall above the worktop and out of reach of small children. Invest in a sharpening steel so you can quickly and simply keep blades in best working condition. Ask a professional if you are unsure how to use it.

Your basic kit should include a range of good-quality saucepans in different sizes so you can cater for varying amounts of food and different types of cooking. Stainless steel pans are a good choice as they are easy to clean. Look for heavy, ground bases as they diffuse the heat evenly and help prevent food sticking and burning. The sides of the pans should be quite high so that food can be stirred and liquid ingredients can be easily added at later stages. Make sure that lids are tight fitting for efficient simmering. Copper pans are more of a rarity these days, but they are attractive to display and a good conductor of heat.

A roasting tin is a must in most kitchens; non-stick tins are coated to resist fat and to ease cleaning. You will also need a frying pan and an omelette pan. To protect the non-stick surface, avoid using metal implements which might scratch and damage the finish. Use instead wood, plastic or carbon fibre utensils.

Steel pans can be expensive but beware of aluminium pans which can affect the flavour and colour of certain foods. Cast-iron casserole dishes are perfect for slow cooking and stews and handsome enough to take to the table. When new, cast-iron should be seasoned before use.

RIGHT: Every kitchen should have a basic set of kitchen tools and utensils that perform specific tasks and are kept within easily accessible range of the cooking area.

LEFT: A magnetic knife holder situated on the wall at the back of the worktop is convenient for cooks, while keeping them out of the reach of small children. **BELOW:** Basic equipment such as a whisk and cheese grater in hardwearing, long-lasting materials is a must for every kitchen – necessary for even the simplest meals. **RIGHT:** Moveable hooks attached to a long, hanging rail allow those frequently used cooking implements and ingredients to be located within easy reach of the cook.

To season, paint the surface with vegetable oil and place the pan in a moderate oven for half an hour. Remove from the oven, leave to cool and then repeat the process twice more. To clean the pan, wipe clean with a paper towel or wash under hot water, but do not use detergent, which will break down the protective coating. Judge the size you will need according to the number of people you regularly cook for, but if in doubt, err on the generous side. Casseroles, in particular, will reduce in bulk as they stew, but the raw ingredients can take up a surprising amount of space.

Wok cooking has become increasingly popular and allows you to cook a healthy stir fry quickly and simply. Some are pre-seasoned which cuts out the process of deep cleaning and repeated heating and oiling. They can also come with a handy round steam rack and domed cover to keep juices in.

Keen cooks will also want adequate baking equipment, – a couple of pudding bowls and cake tins in different sizes, a loaf tin, a pie dish, a soufflé dish, a loose-bottomed flan tin and pastry cutters. Just about everybody needs a large mixing bowl, and a set of weighing scales and measuring jug will ensure you get quantities exactly right.

Small appliances

There are so many desirable small appliances on the market that you may be tempted to buy more than you need. Ask yourself how often you would use a certain machine and assess whether you have the space to store it. Not only that, but some small machines come with a vast range of accessories which can be fiddly and time-consuming to wash, so find out also whether the various parts are dishwasher-proof.

A good food processor can improve and speed up food preparation, and can be used as a blender for soups and smoothies; some also come with a detachable grinder for coffee beans and nuts. However, you should ask yourself whether the tasks for which you would use a bulky food processor could be done more quickly, and with less washing up, using a selection of individual machines instead

or even a good, sharp knife. Perhaps buying a blender would be more useful and less cumbersome than a multifunction food processor?

A toaster is a staple appliance in the kitchen these days, but make sure you choose one that can toast different thicknesses of bread as well as crumpets, muffins and bagels. Have you got time to prepare freshly squeezed orange juice? If so, would you prefer a manual, hand-lever squeezer or a small, efficient electric juicer? Coffee-lovers may want to invest in a state-of-the-art cappuccino and espresso machine (expensive built-in versions are also available); otherwise, a stove-top percolator or cafetière can do the job just as well.

Other specialist machines such as a pasta maker, bread maker, ice-cream maker and yoghurt maker will depend on your cooking habits and expertise as well as your available storage space.

SINKS AND TAPS

Sinks

Even if you have a dishwasher to deal with your stack of dirty dishes, you still need a good kitchen sink to rinse, fill, drain, handwash and prepare food. Choose a sink based on function, space and style. Whether you want one, two or three bowls depends on your work habits, available space and budget. A large single bowl, roomy enough for oversize pans and chopping boards may be enough if you do have a dishwasher, but make sure your largest pan can fit into the bowl easily – take it into showrooms if necessary. However, a double or one-and-a-half bowl (one small bowl between the main sink and drainer) is good for washing and rinsing at the same time. Triple sinks will need lots of worktop space and may incorporate a waste disposal unit in the centre. Round sinks look visually attractive but do not make best use of available space (although they can be a good secondary sink for vegetable preparation), while an L-shaped sink maximises space by fitting into a corner unit. Flexible, multifunction sinks are becoming more popular. These large-capacity sinks can accommodate an enormous amount of crockery, pots and pans, good for large families who do not have a dishwasher or for post-dinner party chaos. For everyday use and smaller loads, the sink's dimensions can be halved using a removable wall divider or bowl insert.

The style of your sink and the material it is made from should fit in with the overall look of your kitchen. Inset sinks are probably the most common type, where the lip of the sink stands a few millimetres above the worktop and is sealed with a waterproof edge. Far more convenient and hygienic are flush-mounted versions which are seamlessly installed with the worktop. There are no edges or joins to harbour dirt or bacteria, and liquids can be wiped straight from the worktop into the sink. Undermounted, rimless sinks are set under stone or wood, while integral sinks are made of the same material as the worktop, most commonly stainless steel or a composite material like Corian, to give a neat, one-piece finish.

To tie in with the trend for unfitted kitchens, freestanding sink units are fast becoming popular. Like something straight out of a commercial kitchen, these modular workstations on legs feature a chunky slab of stainless steel with bowl and drainer on top, and shelf below.

Materials

Stainless steel remains a popular choice for sinks. It is tough, resists rust, corrosion and heat, and can withstand sudden temperature changes. It is also extremely hygienic. Better sinks contain more nickel, giving the sinks a richer lustre, warmer colour, better cleanability and resistance to water spotting and scratches. A high-quality 18/10 grade has 18 per cent chromium and 10 per cent nickel added during manufacture to make the stainless steel rustproof. The thicker the gauge, the quieter and sturdier the sink. An 18 gauge steel is the best choice for domestic use while the thicker 16 gauge is for commercial applications. Thinner 20 and 22 gauges will be noisier, tinnier and could possibly flex with heavy pans. A highly polished finish is more likely to show up scratches than brushed, satin and textured versions. Other metal sinks include white bronze (an alloy of copper, manganese and zinc), brass, sandcast aluminium and copper. Each gives a warmer nuance than steel.

Ceramic sinks have a natural high glaze finish that is functional and good looking. Large, oblong Belfast and farmhouse sinks of porcelain-coated fireclay suit both traditional and modern country kitchens. These sinks can be set on top of kitchen base units or wall-mounted using supporting brackets. Modern-style ceramic sinks with an inset design suit the more contemporary kitchen. Cast-iron sinks with thick layers of porcelain enamel fused on top retain their lustrous finish and sparkle for years with proper care. The smooth, non-porous surface is resistant to chips,

RIGHT: The most successful kitchens mix and match fixtures and fittings to create a unique look. Here a large, oblong Belfast sink is inset into the modern chocolate brown units for a vibrant new spin on the country kitchen.

ABOVE: Limestone is most widely recognised in colours such as soft cream, buff and sand, but here, a pebble-grey limestone worktop is the perfect foil to the double bowl Belfast sink and modern single-lever chrome tap. **RIGHT:** A block of dark greeny-grey Corian has been formed into a deep, rectangular sink with a seamless, one-piece splashback and work surface.

The chunky pale wood legs emphasise the simplicity and solidity of the washstation.
CENTRE RIGHT: The kitchen sink has been transformed into a multifunction preparation centre with sliding chopping boards and a lidded cut-out positioned above a waste bin.
FAR RIGHT: A seamless, one-piece sink and worktop in stainless steel means there are no dirt traps for bacteria.

stains, scratches, soap and food acids while the inherent strength of cast-iron enables the sinks to be made larger and deeper without danger of flexing. They come in as many colours as paint.

Synthetic sinks are made of composite materials containing a mix of resin, acrylic and natural stone particles such as granite and quartz. They are warm to the touch, durable and can resist extremely high temperatures, dents, chips and stains. Basically, the higher the stone content, the tougher the sink. These are available in a wide selection of plain colours and granite effects.

Corian and other solid surface materials are sleek, modern, and can be expensive. Sinks come as an integral bowl moulded seamlessly into a counter of the same material with the option of a carved-out drainer.

A wood sink will lend understated luxury and warmth to any style of kitchen. These are made from teak in simple square designs and are incredibly warm and tactile. The timber reduces the noise of clattering dishes and naturally inhibits bacterial growth, while a laminate teak base prevents leakage.

New innovations include a light-up translucent sink made from tough polymer in a range of zesty colours including lime, lemon and bright pink. It features a touch-sensitive disc that turns the light on or off and anti-bacterial protection.

Sinks are not just for washing dishes. With the help of some extra accessories such as slide-over chopping boards, wire baskets, drainers and colanders, our humble kitchen sink is quickly transformed into a multifunction workstation, which is brilliant for the smaller kitchen.

Taps

These are one of the most hardworking, frequently used elements of your kitchen. With this one item you fill sinks, buckets and saucepans, swill dishes before they go in the dishwasher and rinse hands and vegetables. Kitchen taps are constantly in use, so it is crucial that you select the correct model. Which type of tap is best for you rests with your personal preference and the style of your kitchen. There is a huge choice available including sophisticated, hands-free taps which turn on and off when heat sensors detect your hands underneath. Mixer taps integrate hot and cold water into a single spout, allowing you to get exactly the right temperature. Single-lever versions control the flow and temperature of the water with one easy-to-use lever. Pillar taps keep temperatures separate with two fittings, one for hot and one for cold, while bridge mixers have separate hot and cold taps joined to a central spout by a bar. Both styles look good with traditional sinks such as large Belfast sinks.

A pull-out spray spout with an extendable hose is useful for rinsing pots, pans and dishes before they go into the dishwasher and for washing surfaces around the sink. For someone who suffers from arthritis, lever taps are a good option as they can be turned on with an elbow or forearm. A tall, swan-neck spout facilitates filling tall pots and buckets. To free up space on the sink or worktop wall-mounted taps are a good idea, even better if they have an adjustable spout.

Look for a tap with just a quarter-turn action which can be turned fully on or off with just a 90-degree movement, rather than a full 360 degrees. Also, drip-free ceramic disc technology is far better than a tap that relies on a washer to control the flow of water. Taps cast of solid brass (copper and zinc) will give maximum corrosion resistance, whereas mid-price taps are often made from recycled brass and those at the lower end of the price scale are usually plastic.

Taps come in many finishes including chrome (brushed, matt and high-polish), brass, epoxy coatings (tough, smooth and in many colours), pewter and nickel.

Water filters

If you drink a great deal of bottled water, you may want to install an integral water filter as an alternative. This self-contained unit is housed tucked away under the sink and purifies the cold water as it passes through the system, taking out any sediment, rust, scale and chemicals. Such a three-way tap dispenses hot and cold water (independently or mixed) and has an extra lever on the tap body to operate the purification system. The special ceramic cartridges provide around six months of purified water.

BELOW LEFT: A custom-made triangular sink utilises unused space beneath the kitchen window. It is finished off with a single-lever mixer tap, which controls both the temperature and flow of the water. **BELOW RIGHT:** Two circular stainless steel bowls are undermounted beneath a green stone worktop while a bridge mixer with separate pillar taps a touch of elegance. **RIGHT:** The tactile, earthiness of this thick, pale-toned concrete worktop is offset with a simple stainless steel sink and chrome, swan-neck tap spout.

WASTE DISPOSAL

Waste is an unavoidable by-product of human existence. The problem is that there is so much of it. Even the smallest household produces a staggering amount of rubbish. Regulations on waste disposal vary from country to country. In Germany, residents are required by law to separate rubbish. In the United States, recycling mandates vary from city to city, state to state.

It is estimated that around 25 per cent of household waste is food. For those with a garden or field, compost heaps can be a great way to recycle vegetable leftovers. However, protein waste such as meat, fish and dairy products should not be composted, as they can produce harmful airborne pathogens during putrescence.

Waste disposal units

Most homes in the United States have an electric waste disposer and 80 per cent of all new homes have one fitted. They sit underneath the sink waste outlet and get rid of food scraps including bones, nuts, egg shells and fruit. Food waste is fed into the disposer with water from the cold tap and converted into a fine slush that goes into the drains. Depending where you live, it is then recycled with other organic waste as agricultural fertiliser.

There are no knives or blades in this system. A spinning metal plate pushes the food against a tough grind ring fixed to the wall of the food chamber. The waste is ground safely to fine particles and flushed out through the drainage pipes. Quiet motors have been developed to keep noise to a minimum while compact units leave plenty of storage space under the sink.

There are two types of waste disposal units. A continuous feed model is always open, allowing a steady stream of food waste to be fed into the disposer as it operates. It is controlled by a switch on the wall or work surface. A batch feed will only operate when a special sink plug is inserted into the disposer after the waste has been fed in. Turning the plug starts and stops the disposer; the waste is therefore processed a batch at a time. This is safer for small children and prevents teaspoons from going down the spout, but it is more expensive.

Trash compactors

Trash compactors are more commonly associated with American households, but large families who produce a lot of rubbish may want to consider one.

LEFT: Dedicated storage space is the key to making recycling as effortless as possible. Plastic, stackable bins beneath the worktop is as effective as the most sophisticated waste disposal system.

RIGHT: Separating waste into different categories ready for recycling is environmentally responsible. Semi-transparent PVC storage bins with lids allow you to see what is being stored in each container.

FAR LEFT: An adjoining utility room or porch can be ideal for storing both your rubbish and recycling containers. The rubbish collected can then be easily transported outside for collection or taken to a central recycling depot. **LEFT:** This pull-out waste storage unit has been subdivided into smaller bins for collecting different types of materials.

These trash compactor machines can reduce rubbish to a far more manageable size – less than one-quarter of its original bulk – and compress it into tidy square bundles wrapped in paper sacks. Compactors can either be portable or attached under the worktop and can be used to compress non-biodegradables and packaging materials such as cardboard and plastic containers. They can also be used for recycling purposes if you restrict them to crush only one type of rubbish, aluminium cans or newspapers for instance. However they can be expensive and the compressed bundles can take a long time to decompose. It may be better to flatten cans by stamping on them or using a mechanical press. Either way, aluminium cans take an estimated 80–100 years to degrade and plastic bags 10–20 years. To help minimise the waste that goes into your bin, always try to select products with the least amount of packaging, and reuse containers, bags and other items wherever possible.

Recycling

Separating rubbish into different categories ready for recycling is environmentally responsible. Many households are already required by law to separate waste into paper, biodegradables, glass and metals – and those who are not are encouraged to do so in order to protect the environment.

The key to separating rubbish is creating the space to do so. You should also find the most convenient recycling point. The waste may be collected from your home on a designated day, or you might have to take it to a depot.

Waste sorting systems that fit below the worktop make it extremely easy to organise household waste. These pull-out drawer systems are divided into separate, removable bins for collecting different types of materials. Otherwise make room for stacks of newspapers, magazines and printed matter, and boxes of bottles and glass, either in a garage, shed or spare cupboard. Stash them in containers that can be easily transported to the collection point.

Resources

The preceding sections provided inspiration, ideas and information to help you equip and design your kitchen to your specification. In these pages, we provide more in-depth details of some of the more practical elements, such as questions to ask your supplier when buying a kitchen, crucial safety information and advice on measuring up. There is also a budget planner for you to plan your finances accurately as well as advice on work schedules. Finally, there is a comprehensive list of suppliers as a basis for your research.

BUDGET PLANNER

The cost of a new kitchen will depend on many variables: individual needs, style of life, priorities and budget. The size of the room is another factor, but do bear in mind that the smallest kitchen can cost twice as much as a huge one – it all depends on the quality and cost of fixtures and fittings. Ask yourself how important the kitchen is to you and your family – is it a well-used room, the real hub of family life, or is it somewhere just to reheat the occasional meal. How you use your kitchen will translate into how much you wish to spend on it. The amount you spend must also relate to the value of the property in which the kitchen will live.

However large or small your budget, the most important thing is to stick to it. The best way to keep track of what you've spent and to avoid potential hidden costs is to break down every single element of your project.

What it can cost:

▶ Initial consultation and kitchen plan
▶ Structural work
▶ Rewiring and relocating utilities

▶ Lighting
▶ Heating
▶ Flooring
▶ Kitchen units:
    Cabinets
    Shelving
    Fittings
▶ Handles/knobs
▶ Worktops
▶ Splashback
▶ Sink and taps
▶ Appliances:
    Oven, hob and extractor fan
    Fridge and freezer
    Microwave
    Dishwasher
    Laundry appliances
    Waste disposal unit
▶ Decoration – materials and labour
▶ Delivery of kitchen
▶ Installation of kitchen

By budgeting for these elements, you should be able to avoid hidden costs and stick within budget. If you do go over budget, you can easily rethink certain elements if necessary. For example, you could substitute a very expensive stone floor with a poured and painted concrete one or tackle the decoration yourself rather than hiring a professional. However, never skimp on important costs such as electrician and plumber's fees and the installation of your kitchen.

Before you start, prioritise your needs according to what you will value in a kitchen: don't splash out on a terrazzo worktop if you can't afford to buy a refrigerator. Everyone will have different priorities. A keen cook may sacrifice the luxury of a tumble dryer and chic designer door knobs in favour of a robust, powerful range cooker, whereas large-capacity laundry appliances may be top of the list for big families. Make a list of your priorities and an inventory of what you have in your existing kitchen. You may be able to reuse certain elements or sell on others to raise extra cash for your new purchase. And be realistic, if you haven't got a huge budget, glass surfaces and a built-in steam oven may be out of the question.

BUYER'S QUESTIONNAIRE

Buying a kitchen can be the most expensive purchase you ever make – after your house and car. It's a big financial commitment, so you need to ensure that the money and time you invest will get you the kitchen you want, both in terms of design and function. Of course, budgetary constraints will pay a large part, but whether you're buying a flat-pack kitchen from a DIY store or commissioning a carpenter to make a unique, one-off design tailored specifically to your needs, there are some crucial questions you should ask your potential kitchen retailer before you sign on the dotted line. Be aware that staff at DIY stores will not be as knowledgeable as the kitchen specialists, so you may need to do more research yourself.

Questions to ask

Is the company a member of a recognised trade body? A trade association will give you peace of mind that the business has been checked and approved and can offer protection against bankruptcy or any disputes. Look for logos in a shop window or simply ask.

What does the price include? Ask for a detailed written quotation that covers every aspect of the job including fitting, tiling, flooring and any structural alterations you have discussed. Don't be afraid to question the price if the original quote isn't within your budget. For example, a cheaper worktop material and less expensive appliances may dramatically affect the total.

How much deposit will I have to pay? Nearly all showrooms ask for some sort of deposit – but never pay the full amount when you place your order. A deposit of around 25 per cent is normal, anything higher than 40 per cent is suspicious. And do not sign anything unless you are prepared to honour your side of the sales contract. Some retailers have expensive cancellation clauses.

Is there a free design service? Most showrooms offer this as a free service but check to see that an extra charge isn't added onto your total bill. It is more likely that bespoke designers will charge you for plans.

How long will the job take? Find out when the kitchen is due to arrive and how long it will take to install. Get a written estimate for extra peace of mind.

How strong is the kitchen? Look at showroom cabinets and inspect how sturdy the furniture is. Don't be afraid to pull open drawers and doors and inspect areas that receive the heaviest wear, such as edges and hinges. Find out what the carcases are made of.

Can I see previous installations or speak to previous customers? This is crucial if you are buying a bespoke, tailormade kitchen. Only then can you get an overall feel for the company and fully inspect the workmanship and quality of the units. At the very least, ask to see a portfolio of work.

Do you offer a full aftersales service? Ask if the company offers any written guarantees – against faulty fittings and appliances and shoddy workmanship. If they also installed the kitchen for you, do they inspect when fitting is complete?

Questions a retailer should ask you

It's not only you who should be armed with a list of questions when buying a kitchen. Any reputable retailer should also have myriad questions to find out about your home and lifestyle. Judge a kitchen company by how many of the following you are asked.

When can I make a site visit? Independent retailers and bespoke companies should always visit your home before they give a firm quotation. This way, they can accurately measure up the kitchen, plan the layout and also work out what building work may be required. Be wary of those who do not visit your home. Saying that, it is highly unlikely that larger outlets like DIY stores will offer a site survey, so you need to be prepared with accurate measurements yourself.

What do you like and dislike about your current kitchen? Finding out what works well and what doesn't, can help a retailer to design a kitchen to suit your exact specifications.

What is your budget? There is no point in planning a blow-the-budget kitchen if you haven't got a huge amount of cash to spend. Fixing a budget before the design process begins is crucial. And don't assume that a specialist kitchen shop is an expensive option; a good retailer should be able to work within your budget and still give you the kitchen you want. But bear in mind that bespoke kitchens are a lot pricier.

Lifestyle questions

▶ Who will use the kitchen? Do you have children or pets?
▶ Is anyone in the family elderly or disabled?
▶ Do you want somewhere to eat in the kitchen – a table or breakfast bar? Do you want to hold dinner parties there?
▶ Apart from cooking and preparation, what else is your kitchen used for? Laundry, ironing, homework, entertaining?
▶ What style would you like your kitchen to be? What colours, flooring and wall coverings do you prefer?
▶ How much storage do you need? Do you want open shelving or closed cupboard space, fitted or unfitted?
▶ What kind of appliances do you want? Freestanding or built-in? And what type of fuel do you plan to use?
▶ Are you planning to extend your kitchen? Are there any structural items in place?

SAFETY HINTS AND TIPS

Don't forget the safety aspect of your kitchen. This is a room full of sharp utensils and hot appliances, a lethal combination that can lead to accidents if you aren't vigilant. However, by incorporating a few simple safety precautions into your design, you can avoid potential disasters.

Cooking appliances

▸ Try to buy appliances with built-in safety features such as a child-lock button on hobs that will prevent children turning on the heat by accident.

▸ Gas hobs with a flame-failure device will automatically cut out the gas supply should a pan overboil or if a sudden gust of wind accidentally blows out the flame.

▸ Look out for double- or triple-glazed oven doors, which keep them cool to the touch.

▸ Non-tilt oven shelves (also called telescopic shelves) won't tip over even if you have a heavy casserole dish resting at the end.

▸ Shorten flexes on small appliances or replace with the curly type to prevent children accidentally pulling on any which might overhang the worktop. Never trail flexes across a sink or hob and install electrical switches and power points well away from the water source.

▸ Flank the cooking areas with a heat-resistant worktop material such as stainless steel or granite.

▸ Install cookers and hobs away from windows – draughts may blow out gas flames and curtains may catch fire (unless the hob has a flame-failure device).

Cooling and washing

▸ Look out for fridges and freezers fitted with door alarms to alert you if the door isn't closed properly. Leaving a door open will allow internal temperatures to rise and food to spoil, potentially leading to food poisoning.

▸ Fridges should be set between 0–5°C and freezers at –18°C.

▸ Fridges and freezers should be located away from extreme temperatures so they can work efficiently. Don't locate a fridge-freezer in a garage unless you have a separate thermostat for the freezer, and don't site a fridge next to a heat source such as a radiator or cooker – it will have to over-compensate and use more energy.

▸ Understand the star ratings on your freezer and frozen food. One star means frozen food can be stored for one week; two stars means frozen food can be stored for one month; three stars means frozen food can be stored for three months; and four stars means fresh food can be frozen.

▸ Door locks on washing machines are essential to prevent children pulling them open and crawling inside.

Planning

▸ Consider ergonomics. Don't put the hob and sink at opposite ends of the kitchen with the oven off at a tangent – running across the room with hot, heavy dishes and cooking oils could not only cause havoc, but also potential disasters.

▸ Look after your back by storing heavy items such as casserole dishes and small appliances in base cupboards or shelves and lighter ones like glassware and packets in wall units.

▸ Deep drawers with non-slip bases or an upright peg system will allow crockery to be stored without sliding and crashing about as the drawer is opened and closed.

▸ If the fridge is on the other side of the room to the oven or chopping surface, invest in a mobile chopping block so you can take out all the food you need in one trip. This will help to avoid too many return trips across the room, which will also lower the temperature of the fridge if you are constantly opening and closing the door.

Other considerations

▸ Avoid sharp corners on worktops and replace with a rounded or axis profile.

▸ Good task lighting is crucial – all work surfaces and cooking areas must be well lit.

▸ Fit child locks on any cupboards containing chemicals, cleaning substances, knives or other potentially dangerous objects.

▸ All kitchens should have a fire extinguisher and fire blanket in case of fire.

▸ Choose a non-slip material for floors and wipe up spills immediately.

▸ If paint was applied to a surface in your kitchen before 1980, there is a 50 per cent chance it contains lead. Investigate and replace if necessary.

▸ If you do any deep-fat frying, learn how to put out a fat fire.

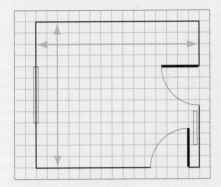
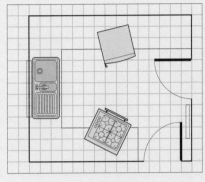
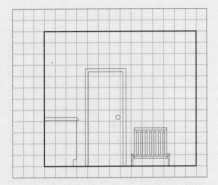

MEASURING UP

Once you have outlined all your requirements to your supplier or designer, the next stage is planning and allocating the space available. Most high street and bespoke companies will accurately measure your kitchen during an initial site visit. However, if you buy your kitchen from a DIY store you will need to provide the measurements of the room and positions of fittings and essential services yourself (see illustration above). Accuracy is vital as fitted rooms will have only small tolerances of error. To do this, you will need metric graph paper, a pencil, ruler and tape measure. Measure in mm or cm, as today's kitchens are all made to metric sizes, and choose a convenient scale to draw up your plans. For example, a 1:20 scale means every square on the graph paper represents 20cm in your kitchen. Consider the following points as you draw up your scale plan:

▶ Measure the width and height of each wall and the distance from the end of the wall to doors and windows.

▶ Draw in the position and size of any permanent fixtures such as doors and windows, showing which way they open and also sill heights.

▶ Measure any projections such as radiators, air vents and pipes – their width, height and distance from wall.

▶ Show the position of gas and water supply points, electrical sockets and fuse boxes.

You may wish to tackle the layout of the kitchen as well. Cut out pieces of paper to scale to represent the sink, cooker and fridge, and arrange them into a work triangle that you think will work for you (see above). Don't position your oven or hob too close to a room door, where someone at the cooker might be hit by the door; neither should you fit wall units above the cooking area unless you fit an extractor fan. To prevent a feeling of claustrophobia, wall units shouldn't be too low, especially around eating areas, and, if you are positioning your fridge or freezer next to the oven, make sure there is adequate insulation between them.

Place the rest of the kitchen on the graph paper. It helps to use tracing paper over the graph paper and draw the emerging floor plan in bold lines so you can see it take shape. Alternatively, you could experiment on your computer using one of the many software programmes that are now available for kitchen design.

Another way to visualise your kitchen layout is to draw each wall to scale (called an elevation, see above). This shows a front view of the cupboards, oven, sink and so on. It will help you to avoid any jarring changes in height and to spot potential problems such as placing the fridge or washing machine in a corner where access will be awkward. Usually the final design is a synthesis of plans and elevations.

You could also label your plans with the colours, materials and appliances you have chosen. So you can keep a track of the cost, choose a variety of products and materials and label them 'good', 'better', 'best' and 'the ultimate'. This way you can easily scale back to control costs by substituting an expensive item for something less pricey: for example, replacing granite worktops with a laminate look-alike.

WORK SCHEDULE

Once you've chosen and ordered your new kitchen, it is essential that you put together a work schedule, particularly if the room is having a complete overhaul. Do you know when the tiles are arriving, for instance, and should the flooring go down before the units are installed? However large or small, a new kitchen means disruption and inconvenience to your daily routine so preparation is key.

Before you start

A good-quality kitchen installation may take around one to two weeks, but if you've chosen a bespoke, tailormade design with extensive redecoration and reconfiguring of space, expect disruption to last up to 14 weeks. You may need to set up a temporary kitchen in another part of the house. If so, make sure the room has access to water and keep portable appliances such as an electric kettle and microwave to hand.

The kitchen must be completely cleared of everything prior to installation. Pack up everything that won't be used in your temporary kitchen, then label the boxes and store out of the way. As well as foodstuffs, remove drawers, spice racks, clocks, curtains and ornaments, and allocate good storage beforehand to minimise clutter. Place a protective sheet over existing floor coverings and anything that must remain in place while the work goes on. If you've chosen a rigid kitchen (as opposed to a flat-pack version that will arrive in boxes) make sure you have adequate floor space for it to stand – ideally, not impeding the installation area itself. Also, do not forget to make arrangements for the disposal of rubbish that will accumulate during the work. If you need to hire a skip, do so in plenty of time and check whether you need to obtain a permit from your local authority if the skip is standing directly on the

road outside your house, instead of a private driveway. And finally you may wish to advise neighbours of any major building work that is about to take place.

Removing appliances

Before removing any major appliances, turn off all utilities. Remember that the law in many countries, including the UK, requires a specified professionally qualified body to install gas appliances. If you are unsure about electricity, call in a qualified electrician. Use carpet samples or pieces of cardboard to slide appliances out of position – it will also help to protect the floor from gouges or scratches. Most refrigerators need only to be unplugged – a fridge or freezer can simply be plugged into a socket in another room, without even emptying. If it has an ice maker, you will need to locate the water supply valve (usually under the sink) and shut it off before disconnecting the supply tube. Don't stock the fridge or freezer if your electricity supply is going to be cut off.

Plumbing matters

Depending on what type of 'fit' you choose, your team of installers may also strip out your old kitchen. If not, disconnect the sink before you tackle the units. Shut off the water supply at the valves below the sink and turn the taps on to drain the water lines. Then remove the clips underneath the sink that secure it to the worktop. Old cast iron sinks are much heavier than stainless steel or porcelain and will need an extra pair of hands when removing it.

Removing old cabinets

Next stage is the removal of worktops and cabinets. Remove the emptied drawers and take off the doors from all the cabinets, then

unscrew the worktop from underneath the base units. If it has been glued down, you may need to use a crowbar to lever the worktop off, but remember to protect the wall by sliding a piece of wood between the wall and the crowbar. Tackle the base units first so it will be easier to get underneath the wall cabinets. Base units are usually attached to each other through the sides of the cabinet front and to the back wall using screws (although older types may be nailed in place). Remove all the screws and then lift the cabinet away from the wall. The wall cabinets are attached to each other and the wall in a similar way – remove the screws and the cabinets will come out.

Making good

Once the kitchen is cleared, this is a good time to undertake any preparatory work. If you need to relocate/add electrical outlets, water or waste or gas pipes, or if extensive structural work is included in your plans, it should take place now. Make sure you schedule contractors in advance. Otherwise, while there are no cabinets or appliances in the kitchen, it is the ideal time to patch and repair walls. You can even apply a primer and first coat of paint.

Floors

If you are planning to replace the floor covering, it is best to do so before the new cabinets are installed. This way, it will run from wall to wall, underneath the cabinets. Hardwood and ceramic tiles are always laid before cabinets are installed as they will raise the height of the floor, although vinyl flooring can be laid after the cabinets are in place. It is important to patch and repair an existing floor if the new floor is being laid directly on top to ensure a smooth surface.

Sample work schedule

1 Clear the kitchen and store everything you don't need in labelled boxes. If necessary, set up a temporary kitchen in a nearby room. Make arrangements for the disposal of rubbish.

2 Turn off the utilities and remove appliances – call in the professionals if you are unsure.

3 Demolition phase. Disconnect plumbing and remove cabinets. If you are planning to donate or sell your old kitchen, have a place ready for the cabinets to go as you take them out.

4 Once the kitchen is clear, major structural work should take priority. Ask for a written schedule of work from all the tradesmen.

5 If there is damp treat it now.

6 Wiring, plumbing and gas installation must be completed next.

7 Electric wiring for lights and wall sockets should be done before any plastering.

8 Repair walls and apply primer and first coat of paint.

9 If you are upgrading the floor covering, do so before the new cabinets are installed. Vinyl flooring can be laid after the cabinetry is in place.

10 Your room is now ready for the installation team to fit the new kitchen.

Suppliers List

Kitchens Design: Bespoke & Classic

ANDREW MACINTOSH
462–464 Chiswick High Road
London W4
020 8995 8333

BROWNS KITCHENS
85 White Hart Lane
London SW13 0PW
020 8878 9944

CHALON UK
Hambridge Mill, Hambridge
Somerset TA10 0BP
01458 254600
www.chalon.com

CLIVE CHRISTIAN
164 Brompton Road
London SW3 1HW
020 7581 9200
www.clivechristian.com

CRABTREE KITCHENS
17 Station Road
London SW13 0LF
020 8392 6955
www.crabtreekitchens.co.uk

HARVEY JONES
0800 9172340

JOHN LEWIS OF
HUNGERFORD
Park Street, Hungerford
Berkshire RG17 0EF
01488 688100
www.john-lewis.co.uk

JOHNNY GREY
Fyning Copse, Rogate
Petersfield, Hampshire
GU31 5DH
01730 821424
www.johnnygrey.co.uk

KEITH GRAY & CO
Great Priory Farm
Panfield, Braintree
Essex CM7 5BQ
01376 324590
www.keith-gray.co.uk

MARK WILKINSON
FURNITURE
Overton House, High Street
Bromham, Wiltshire
SN15 2HA
01380 850004
www.mwf.com

MOWLEM & CO
555 Kings Road
London SW6 2EB
020 7610 6626

NEWCASTLE FURNITURE
COMPANY
Green Lane Buildings
Pelaw, Tyne & Wear
NE10 0UW
0191 438 1342
www.newcastlefurniture.com

PLAIN ENGLISH
The Tannery, Combs
Stowmarket, Suffolk
IP14 2EN
01449 774028

ROBINSON AND CORNISH
Southay House, Oakwood Close
Roundswell, Barnstaple
Devon EX31 3NJ
01271 329300
www.robinsonandcornish.co.uk

ROUNDHOUSE DESIGN
020 7428 9955
www.roundhousedesign.com

SHAKER
72/73 Marylebone High Street
London W1U 5JW
020 7935 9461
www.shaker.co.uk

SMALLBONE
105-109 Fulham Road,
London SW3 6RL
020 7581 9989
www.smallbone.co.uk

UNDERWOOD KITCHENS
Lawn Farm Business Centre
Grendon Underwood
Buckinghamshire
HP18 0QX
01296 771800
www.underwood-
kitchens.co.uk

Modern & Modular
ALNO
Unit 10, Hampton Farm
Industrial Estate
Hampton Road West,
Hanworth, Middlesex
TW13 6DB
020 8898 4781
www.alno.co.uk

ARCLINEA
at Humphersons at Heal's
196 Tottenham Court Road
London W1
020 7636 1390

BOFFI
Alternative Plans
9 Hester Road, London
SW11 4AN
020 7228 6460
www.alternative-plans.co.uk

BULTHAUP
37 Wigmore Street, London
W1U 1PP
020 7495 3663
www.bulthaup.com

FK&F
19 Carnwath Road, London
SW6 3HR
020 7736 6458

HABITAT
0845 6010740
www.habitat.net

IKEA
020 8208 5600
www.ikea.co.uk

MAGNET
0800 192192
www.magnet.co.uk

MIELE
Fairacres, Marcham Road
Abingdon, Oxon
OX14 1TW
01235 554455
www.miele.co.uk

NOMAD
01582 670369

PLAIN AND SIMPLE
KITCHENS
1 Filmer Studios, 75 Filmer Road
London SW6 7JF
020 7731 2530
www.plainandsimplekitchens.com

POGGENPOHL
Silbury Court
368 Silbury Boulevard
Milton Keynes MK9 2AF
01908 247612

RATIONAL
24–28 Crossway House
High Street, Bracknell, Berks
RG12 1DA
01344 455800
www.rational.de

SIEMATIC UK
Osprey House, Rookery Court
Primett Roa, Stevenage
Herts SG1 3EE
01438 369251
www.siematic.co.uk

VARENNA
Chelsea Harbour Design Centre
London SW10 0XE
020 7795 0708
www.varenna.co.uk

VIADUCT
1/10 Summer's Street
London EC1R 5BD
020 7278 8456
www.viaduct.co.uk

Ceramic Tiles and Splashbacks
CRITERION TILES
196 Wandworth Bridge Road
London SW6 2UF
020 7736 9610
www.criterion-tiles.co.uk

NATURAL TILE
150 Church Road
Redfield, Bristol BS5 9HN
0117 941 3707
www.naturaltile.co.uk

WELBECK TILES
Unit 3, Tan Gallop
The Welbeck Estate, Worksop
Nottinghamshire S80 3LW
01909 476539
www.welbeck-tiles.co.uk

Flooring
Rubber, linoleum & vinyl
AMTICO
Kingfield Road, Coventry
CV6 5AA
024 7686 1590
www.amtico.co.uk

DALSOUPLE
PO Box 140 Bridgwater
Somerset TA5 1HT
01278 727777
www.dalsouple.com

FORBO NAIRN (MARMOLEUM)
PO Box 1, Kirkcaldy
Fife KY1 2SB
01592 643 777
www.forbo-nairn.co.uk

Tile and stone
FIRED EARTH
Twyford Mill, Oxford Road
Adderbury, Banbury
Oxfordshire OX17 3HP
01295 812088
www.firedearth.com

PARIS CERAMICS
583 Kings Road
London SW6 2EH
020 7371 7778
www.parisceramics.com

KIRKSTONE (see worktops)

STEVE CHARLES & CO
(by appointment only)
020 7384 4424
www.stevecharles.com

STONE AGE
19 Filmer Road
London SW6 7BU
020 7385 7954
www.estone.co.uk

WORLD'S END TILES
Silverthorne Road, Battersea
London SW8 3HE
020 7819 2100
www.worldsendtiles.co.uk

Wood
JUNCKERS (see worktops)

KALFLOOR BAMBOO
Kiani House, Kitling Road
Knowsley, Prescot
Merseyside L34 9HN
0151 549 0828

LASSCO FLOORING
41 Maltby Street
London SE1 3PA
020 7237 4488
www.lassco.co.uk

SOLID FLOOR
53 Pembridge Road
London W11 3HG
020 7221 9166
www.solidfloor.co.uk

Sinks and Taps
ASTRACAST
PO Box 20, Birstall
West Yorkshire, WF17 9XD
01924 477466
www.astracast.co.uk

ATRIFLO
Orwell Close
Fairview Industrial Park
Rainham, Essex RM13 8UB
01708 526361
www.avilion.co.uk

BLANCO
Oxgate Lane, Cricklewood
London NW2 7JN
020 8452 3399

DORNBRACHT
www.dornbract.com

FRANKE
East Park, MIOC, Styal Road
Manchester M22 5WB
0161 436 6280
www.franke.co.uk

IN-SINK-ERATOR
(waste disposal systems)
Chelmsford Road,
Great Dunmow, Essex
CM6 1LP
01371 873073
www.insinkerator.com

POLISHED METAL
PRODUCTS
Devauden Green, Chepstow
Monmouthshire, NP16 6PL
01291 650455
www.sinks.co.uk

SCHOCK UK LTD
Unit 238, Walton Summit
Centre, Bamber Bridge,
Preston, Lancs PR5 8AL
01772 337733
www.schock.de

Worktops
Man-made composites
CD (UK)
Whitehall Buildings, Whitehall
Road, Leeds LS12 1BG
0113 244 5337

CORIAN
0800 962116
www.corian.com

WHITEHALL WORKSURFACES
Exhibition House, Grape Street,
Leeds LS10 1BX
0113 2444892

Stainless steel
GEC ANDERSON
01442 826999

Wood
BORDERCRAFT
Old Forge, Peterchurch
Herefordshire HR2 0SD
01981 550251

DANTOPS
38 The Vintners
Temple Farm Industrial Estate
Southend on Sea, Essex
SS2 5RZ
01702 468241
www.spekva.com

JUNCKERS
Wheaton Court Commercial
Centre, Wheaton Road,
Witham, Essex CM8 3UJ
01376 517512
www.junckers.co.uk

Laminate
DUROPAL
131 St Peter's Court
Chalfont St Peter
Bucks SL9 9QJ
01753 886557

FORMICA
Coast Road,North Shields
Tyne & Wear NE29 8RE
0191 259 3512
www.formica-europe.com

Stone
DIESPEKER MARBLE &
TERRAZZO
020 7358 0160

J&R MARBLE
020 8539 6471
www.jrmarble.co.uk

KIRKSTONE QUARRIES LTD
Skelwith Bridge, Ambleside
Cumbria LA22 9NN
015394 33296
www.kirkstone.com

WELSH SLATE
01766 831511

Glass
OZONE
020 7351 0066
www.ozoneglass.co.uk

BLU
The Barn, Pilmore Lane
Watchfield, Somerset TA9 4LB
01278 793644
www.blu.co.uk

Concrete
PAUL DAVIES DESIGN
020 8541 0838

TOTEM DESIGN
020 7243 0692

Small Appliances & Accessories

BRABANTIA
Blackfriars Road, Nailsea
Bristol BS48 4SB
01275 810600

THE CONRAN SHOP
Michelin House
81 Fulham Road
London SW3 6RD
020 7589 7401
www.conran.co.uk

CUCINA DIRECT
020 8246 4300
www.cucinadirect.co.uk

DAVID MELLOR
4 Sloane Square
London SW1 8EE
020 7730 4259

DIVERTIMENTI
44 Fulham Road
London SW6 6HH
020 7581 8065
www.divertimenti.co.uk

ELIZABETH DAVID COOKSHOP
3 North Row
The Market
Covent Garden
London WC2E 8RA
020 7836 9167

GILL WING COOKSHOP
192 Upper Street
London N1 1RQ

HABITAT
(see kitchen furniture)

ICTC
3 Caley Close
Sweet Briar Road
Norwich NR3 2BU
01603 488019
www.ictc.co.uk

JERRY'S HOME STORE
163-167 Fulham Road
London SW3 6SN
020 7581 0909
www.jerryshomestore.com

MORPHY RICHARDS
08450 777700
www.morphyrichards.co.uk

OCEAN
0870 2426283
www.oceanuk.com

SUMMERHILL & BISHOP
100 Portland Road
London W11 4LN
020 7221 4566

WARING
Unit 2 Fleming Way
Worton Road, Isleworth
TV7 6EU
020 8232 1800

Appliances

AGA-RAYBURN
Station Road, Ketley
Telford, Shropshire TF1 5AQ
08457 626147
www.aga-rayburn.co.uk

AMERICAN APPLIANCE
CENTRE
5 The Dencora Centre
Dundee Way, Enfield
Middlesex EN3 7SX
020 8443 9999
www.american-appliance.co.uk

BUYERS & SELLERS
120–122 Ladbroke Grove
London W10 5NE
0845 085 5585

FALCON PROFESSIONAL
KITCHEN RANGES
PO Box 37, Foundry Loan
Larbert, Stirlingshire
FK5 4PL
01324 554221
www.glynwed.com

GAGGENAU UK
Grand Union House
Old Wolverton Road
Old Wolverton, Milton Keynes
Buckinghamshire MK12 5PT
01908 328360
www.gaggenau.com

MIELE (see Kitchen Furniture)

NEFF
Grand Union House
Old Wolverton Road
Wolverton, Milton Keynes
Buckinghamshire MK12 5PT
0990 133090
www.neff.co.uk

THE RANGE COOKER CO
Range House
281 Bristol Avenue
Blackpool FY2 0JF
01253 471111
www.rangecooker.co.uk

Useful Addresses

CORGI
01256 372300
www.corgi-gas.com

DISABLED LIVING
FOUNDATION
380-384 Harrow Road
London W9 2HU
020 7289 6111
www.dlf.org.uk

THE INSTITUTE OF PLUMBING
64 Station Lane, Hornchurch
Essex RM12 6NB
01708 472791
www.plumbers.org.uk

THE KITCHEN SPECIALISTS
ASSOCIATION
12 Top Barn Business Centre
Holt Heath, Worcester
WR6 6NH
01905 621787
www.ksa.co.uk

ROYAL INSTITUTE OF
BRITISH ARCHITECTS
66 Portland Place
London W1N 4AD
020 7580 5533
www.architecture.com

ROYAL INSTITUTE OF
CHARTERED SURVEYORS
020 7222 7000
www.rics.org.uk

SALVO
01890 820333
www.salvo.co.uk
(to find your nearest
architectural salvage yard)

Access routes 21–2, 26,
   213
aluminium 145, 150, 172, 186,
   191, 207
ambient lighting 122
anti-bacterial products 139,
   201
appliances 170–207
   colour 65, 69
   cooking 174–87
   disabled/elderly people 43
   maintenance manuals 59
   modular 49, 175
   planning 26, 29, 211, 213
   professional 102
   recycling 46, 47, 102
   removal 214
   small 26, 197
   small kitchens 88
   stainless steel 98, 172, 179,
      186, 191
   storage 27, 154, 194
Arad, Ron 69
architects 18, 21–2, 36, 40
architectural features 18, 21,
   26, 211

Bamboo 44, 96, 149
barbeques 108, 176
basement kitchens 21, 22
Berke, Deborah 53
bespoke kitchens 58, 59, 62,
   146, 211
blackboards 20, 72, 82, 147
Bourdain, Anthony 98, 101
breakfast bar 28, 165
budget 19, 21, 40, 58, 146,
   210, 211, 213
building regulations 22, 40
butcher's block 49, 95–6, 132
buying a kitchen 40, 57–9,
   211, 216–19

Carpet 145
ceramic hobs 172, 182, 183

ceramic sinks 72, 95, 198–
   201
children
   inclusive kitchen 77, 82
   kitchen use 8, 14, 24, 35
   safety 26, 183, 212
   universal design 42
chopping boards 29, 37, 49,
   132, 157, 201
colour
   accent 78
   choice 65, 67–75, 95, 96
   delineating areas 70, 75, 78
   lighting 123
   planning 21, 40
   small kitchens 88
   unifying element 78
composite materials 136–7,
   198, 200, 201
compost heap 45, 204
computer planning 40, 58, 213
concealed kitchen 15, 85, 165
concrete
   flooring 144
   island units 119
   worktops 138–9, 165, 203
cookers 174–83
   see also ventilation
   barbeque 108, 176
   finish 172
   location 27, 29, 36, 43
   professional 102
   safety 26, 43, 129, 132, 183,
      212
   side-opening 42, 43
   size 29, 175
cork flooring 145
corners 26, 29, 88, 157, 212
country kitchens 69, 93, 95
cupboards 146–51
   see also storage space
   corners 88, 157
   lighting 122, 147
   painting 150
   professional kitchen 101

removing old 214, 215
   size 29, 146
   small kitchens 88
   tall 27, 29, 157
   updating doors 21, 146

Decoration 62, 66–75,
   126–9, 214, 215
design service 40, 58, 211, 213
   see also planning/design
disabled people 42–3, 186,
   202, 211
dishwashers 29, 43, 173, 192
dividers 162–9
DIY kitchens 57, 58, 211, 213,
   216–19
doors
   cupboard 21, 146, 148–51
   kitchen 26, 88, 104, 107,
      110
downlighters 122, 123, 125
drawers 147–8, 154, 156, 212

Eating areas
   demarcation 70, 75, 78,
      162–5, 167
   outdoor 108
   planning 13–14, 24, 211,
      213
eco-friendly kitchens 44–5,
   124, 129, 144
elderly people 42–3, 186, 211
electricity
   see also lighting
   cookers 176, 180, 183
   planning 54, 59, 214, 215
   safety 26, 54, 212
   sockets 26, 54
energy efficiency 124, 191,
   192, 193, 212
ergonomics 27–34, 42–3, 85,
   212
exotic influences 95–7
extractor fans 26, 29, 57, 82,
   122, 147, 183–5

Fibre optic lighting 124
finishes 118, 126–31
fire 26, 129, 132, 212
fittings 170–207
flexibility 17, 50, 121, 125
flooring 140–5
   delineating areas 24, 69, 78,
      118
   indoor/outdoor link 104
   replacing 214, 215
   safety 26, 212
fluorescent lighting 122, 123,
   124
fridges/freezers 188–91
   location 27, 29, 35, 212
   reconditioned 44, 46
   safety/efficiency 212
   stainless steel 98, 172, 191
function 8–15, 19, 24, 63, 172

Galley kitchen 28, 31
garden
   access 15, 22, 63, 104, 107
   home-grown produce 108,
      110
   outdoor cooking 104–14
gas
   appliance removal 214, 215
   cookers 15, 176, 180–3
   safety 26, 54, 212
glass
   bricks 31, 125, 128
   ceramic hobs 172, 182, 183
   doors 146, 150
   screens 165
   shelves 57, 96, 98
   splashbacks 28, 98, 134
   tiles 129
   walls 106, 107, 112, 115
   worktops 134
granite 135, 136, 142, 213
guests, seating 28, 34, 35

Hagelin, Jan and Ann 158
halogen lights 122, 123–4

halogen rings 183
heating, planning 55
Heinze, Winfried 110
hobs
   ceramic 172, 182, 183
   concealed 37
   electric 183
   gas 176, 183
   safety 43, 212, 213
hygiene 132, 139, 201

Inclusive kitchen 76–83
indoor/outdoor kitchen 104–15
induction hobs 183
installation 59, 211, 214
island units
   concrete 119
   delineating areas 35, 75,
     162–5
   lighting 122
   modular kitchen 46, 49, 51
   planning and design 34, 41
   professional 102, 112
   split-level 18, 162
   ventilation system 29

Knives 98, 102, 194, 196

L-shaped kitchen 32, 78
laboratory-style 12, 18
lacquers 150
laminates 137–8, 148, 150
Lang, George 8
larder 38, 95, 157
laundry equipment
   choice 172, 183
   location 26, 29, 82, 213
   safety 212
   wooden worktops 132
layout
   ergonomics 22, 27–9, 35,
     42–3
   galley kitchen 28, 31
   island kitchen 34
   L-shaped kitchen 32

scale plans 40, 58, 213
single-line 30
U-shaped kitchen 33, 36–9
LED (light-emitting diodes) 124
level changes 78, 82, 83
lifestyle 63, 211
light
   and colour 69–70, 123
   natural 21, 24, 26, 31, 88,
     121
lighting 121–5
   cabinets 122, 147
   control systems 125
   energy-saving bulbs 124
   fittings 124–5
   inclusive kitchen 82
   multi-function kitchen
     121–2
   outdoor eating 108
   planning 54, 121
   small kitchen 88
limestone 136, 142, 168
linoleum 101, 144
location of kitchen 21
loft living
   inclusive kitchen 76
   kitchen division 166–9
   kitchen storage 158–61
   mixing materials 130–1
   planning/design 14, 22, 53
   professional kitchen 101

Marble 29, 132, 133, 136,
   142, 143
materials
   alternatives 58, 210, 213
   eco-friendly 44–5, 124, 129
   finishes 118, 126–31
   mixing 118, 130–1, 132
   natural 44, 70, 95, 144, 145
   quality 57, 58, 59, 146, 211
measuring up 40, 58, 211, 213
metal
   appliances 98, 172, 179,
     186, 191

cupboards 150
   flooring 144, 145
   shelves 115, 154
   sinks 198, 201
   worktops 132, 134–5
microwaves 43, 184, 186
mobile units 42, 43, 46, 101,
   165
modular kitchen 46–53
mood lighting 123, 125
Morgan, Nicole 90
mosaic tiles 129, 138, 142
moving house 21, 49
multi-function ovens 180, 187
multi-generational design
   42–3
multi-purpose uses
   see also open-plan designs
   inclusive kitchen 76–83
   kitchen role 8, 13–14, 24

Needs, evaluating 26, 40, 58
notice board 20, 72, 82, 147

Open-plan designs
   see also loft living
   delineating areas 70, 75,
     78–81
   inclusive kitchen 76–83
   lighting 121
   planning 13–14, 22, 50, 53
   screens/dividers 162–9
outdoor eating 104–15
ovens 174–83, 187, 212, 213

Paint 126–7
   cabinets 150
   eco-friendly 44–5
   flooring 70, 140
   lead-based 26, 212
   work schedule 214, 215
pantry 157
Parkinson, Andrew 98
pastry making 29, 132
pattern 70, 72–3

planning and design 16–59
   see also layout
   budget 19, 21, 40, 58, 210,
     211, 213
   buyer's questionnaire 211
   determining priorities 24–6
   ergonomics 27–34, 43
   location 21–2
   professional advice 19, 21,
     22, 36, 40, 58
planning permission 22, 40
plans, scale 40, 58, 213
plaster 96, 126, 128
plastics 70, 165, 201, 207
plinths 88, 148
plumbing 29, 54, 59, 214
professional advice 19, 21, 22,
   36, 40, 58, 211
professional kitchen 12, 85,
   98–103
pyrolave 136

Quotations 58, 59, 211

Range cookers 36, 95, 174–
   7, 182
recycling
   appliances 46, 47, 102
   furniture 44, 46, 53
   waste disposal 45, 204–7
Rensch, Nico 158
retailers 40, 57–9, 211, 216
Richards, Dominic 167
Rogers, Richard 75
role of kitchen 8–15, 19, 24,
   63
rubber flooring 20, 144, 145

Safety
   cookers 26, 43, 129, 132,
     183, 212
   planning 26, 54, 82, 212
   screens 94, 162–9
scullery 95
services 54, 59

serving hatch 66, 162, 165
shelves
  see also storage space
  disabled people 43
  displays 18, 53, 154, 155
  glass 57, 96, 98
  stainless steel 115, 154
  visual demarcation 165
  wrap-round 38
single-line layout 30, 47, 85, 86
sinks 198–204
  Belfast 72, 95, 198–9
  disabled people 43
  location 27, 29, 35, 212
  materials 134, 198, 201
  removal 214
size of kitchen 13, 19, 22, 24, 63
skylight 25, 26, 107, 108, 123, 125
slate 131, 136, 139, 142, 157
small kitchens
  layout 84–91
  planning 22, 27, 46, 63
solid surfaces 136–7, 198, 200, 201
splashbacks 132–9
  glass 28, 98
  illuminated 121
  stone 136, 139
  tiled 138
  windows 124
spotlights 121, 122, 125
stainless steel
  appliances 12, 15, 98, 172, 179, 186, 191
  kitchen units 150
  shelves 115, 154
  sinks 198, 201
  splashbacks 134
  worktops 12, 132, 134–5
steaming 180, 183, 186, 187
Stefan, Misha 90
stone
  composites 136–7

flooring 44, 70, 95, 107, 140, 142, 157
  shelves 94
  worktops 70, 106, 107, 133, 135–7, 168
storage space 152–61
  see also cupboards; shelves
  concealed 158–61
  country kitchens 95
  disabled people 43
  height 29
  inclusive kitchen 82
  mobile units 42, 43, 46
  open-plan 18, 154, 155
  planning 26, 27, 154, 211
  professional kitchen 101–2
  recycling bins 204, 205
  small kitchens 85, 86, 87
  utensils 18, 154, 155, 197, 212
  vegetables 38, 154
  vernacular kitchen 95, 96
  wall-mounted 26, 53, 212, 213
strip lighting 122, 123, 124
structural alterations 21, 22, 215
style
  choosing 62–3, 67, 172
  planning 15, 21, 26, 40, 58, 211
suppliers 216–19

Tables, pull-down 31, 90, 137
taps 43, 201–3
task lighting 121, 122, 125, 212
technology 172, 180, 189, 191, 193, 201
terrazzo flooring 144
texture 70, 130
themed kitchens 95–7
tiles
  flooring 101, 129, 141–3
  splashbacks 138

wall 93, 96, 129
  worktops 138
tool kit 59
top glazing 108, 125
track lighting 122, 124–5
tumble dryers 193
tungsten bulbs 122
Turvil, Steve 36

U-shaped kitchen 33, 36–9
unfitted kitchens 46–53
universal design 42–3
users 14, 24, 63, 211
utensils
  basic equipment 194–7
  selection 98, 101, 102, 172
  storage 18, 154, 155, 197, 212

Value of kitchen 21, 210
ventilation
  ducting 26, 101, 183–4
  extractor fans 82, 122, 147, 183–5
  planning/design 26, 29, 57
  windows 82, 212
vernacular style 12, 92–7
vinyl flooring 144–5, 215

Wallpaper 129
walls
  finishes 126–9
  lights 125
  painting schedule 214, 215
  wall units 26, 212, 213
washing *see* laundry equipment
waste disposal 204–7, 214
water filters 202
white 67–71, 96, 140, 158–61
windows
  near cookers 36, 212
  outdoor link 35, 106, 107
  planning/design 26, 82
  as splashbacks 124

wine storage 117, 153, 157
wok cooking 183, 197
wood
  country kitchens 93, 95
  doors 148–9
  eco-friendly 44, 129
  flooring 44, 140, 141
  painting 150
  panelling 128, 129
  sinks 201
  texture 70
  walls 128, 129
  worktops 38, 44, 132
work schedule 214–15
work triangle 27–35, 43, 85
worktops 132–9
  height 29, 43
  planning 27, 29
  removing old 214
  safety 26, 212
  small kitchens 88
  temporary 14, 42, 88, 137

Zinc 135, 150

ACKNOWLEDGEMENTS

The publisher would like to thank the following photographers, agencies and architects for their kind permission to reproduce the photographs in this book:

1 Hotze Eisma/Taverne Agency;2 Verne Fotografie; 3-4 Tom Nagy/La Casa de Marie Claire/Picture Press (Stoeppler + Stoeppler Architekten BDA); 6 left Patrik Engquist (Architect: John Pawson); 6 right Winfried Heinze/Conran Octopus; 7 left Lisa Linder/House & Garden/The Condé Nast publications Ltd (Designer:Olga Polizzi); 7 centre & right Winfried Heinze/Conran Octopus; 8-9 Anthony Browell; 10 David Woolley/ Elle Decoration (Architect: Ken Shuttleworth); 12 left Marie Pierre Morel/Stylist:Christian Puech/Marie Claire Maison; 12 right Hotze Eisma/ Taverne Agency; 13 left Eduardo Munzo/The Interior Archive (Architect: David Mikhail); 13 right Chris Gascoigne/ View (Fletcher Priest Architects); 14 Designer: Norbert Wangen; 15 left Henry Wilson/The Interior Archive (Architect:Voon Yee Wong); 15 right Rien Bazen/'Tile Kitchen' design: Arnout Visser, Peter van der Jagt & Erik Jan Kwakkel, 'Handy Burner' design: Peter vander Jagt, both for for Droog Design, 2001; 16 Patrik Engquist (Architect: John Pawson); 18 left Clive Frost; 18-19 Nigel Noyes; 19 right Ken Hayden/Red Cover (Designer: Jonathan Reed); 20 Minh & Wass; 22 Jennifer Cawley; 23 Victoria Gomez/Living etc/IPC Syndication; 24-25 Stefano Azario/Elle Decoration; 25 right Pia Tryde/Homes & Garden/IPC Syndication; 26 Bulthaup; 27 Verity Welstead/Red Cover; 28 above Tim James/View (Architect: Julian Arendt Associates); 28 below Jake Fitzjones/Red Cover (Fulham Kitchens); 30 Jean-Francois Jaussaud; 31 Jennifer Cawley; 32 Patrik Engquist; 33 Guy Obijn; 34 Jennifer Cawley; 35 Verne Fotografie; 36-39 Robin Chanda (Stephen Turvil Architects); 41 Stellan Herner; 42 left Richard Powers; 42 right Giulio Oriani/Vega MG; 44-45 James Mitchell/Red Cover; 45 right Tom Scott (Azman Owen Architects); 46 left Ray Main/Mainstream; 46 right Gianni Basso/Vega MG; 47 above Dennis Gilbert/View (Blanel Architects); 47 below Daniel Hertzell; 48-49 Peter Cook/View (Architect: Magyar Marsoni); 49 left Andreas von Einsiedel/Red Cover; 49 right Richard Powers; 50 above Tim Clinch/The Interior Archive (Designer: Henry Brougham); 50 below left Graham Atkins-Huges/Red Cover; 50 below right Jan Baldwin; 51 James Morris/Axiom Photographic Agency; 52-53 Antoine Bootz/Stylist: D. Rozensztroch/Marie Claire Maison (Architect: Deborah Berke); 53 Paul Ryan/International Interiors (Architect: Deborah Berke); 55 Winfried.Heinze/ Conran Octopus; 56 Guy Obijn; 57 left Tim Young/Living etc/IPC Syndication; 57 right Jean-Francois Jaussaud; 61 Winfried Heinze/Conran Octopus; 62 Deidi von Schaewen (Designer:Jeff Sayre); 63 Kim Sayer/Red Cover; 64 Grazia Branco/Iketrade; 65 Patrik Engquist (Architect: Claessons, Koivisto & Rune); 66 Ray Main/Mainstream (Designer:Andrew Martin); 67 left Ray Main/Mainstream (Designer:Andrew Martin); 67 right Jan Baldwin; 68 above left Eduardo Munzo/The Interior Archive; 68 below left Verity Welstead/ Red Cover; 68-69 Luke White/Elle Decoration; 70 Deidi von Schaewen; 71 left Graham Atkins-Hughs/Red Cover; 71 right Per Gunnarsson/Stylist: Annette Ekjord; 72 above Richard Glover/View (Interior Designer: Deborah Francis); 72 below Per Gunnarsson/Stylist:Annelie Törngren; 73 Minh & Wass; 74- 75 Winfried Heinze/Red Cover; 76 Jan Baldwin; 77 Gianni basso/Vega MG; 78 Peter Cook/View (Tugman Architects); 79 Verne Fotografie; 80-81 Eduardo Munzo/The Interior Archive (Architect: Seth Stein); 80 below Giulio Oriani/Vega MG; 81 below Verity Welstead/Red Cover; 82 Winfried Heinze/Red Cover; 83 Patrik Engquist; 84 Eric Morin/World of Interiors; 85 above Christoph Kicherer (Architect:Briffa Phillips); 85 below Grazia Branco/Iketrade; 86 left Architect: Nico Rensch; 86 right Giulio Oriani/Vega MG; 87 Per Gunnarsson/Stylist:Annelie Törngren; 88 left Giorgio Possenti/Vega MG; 88 right Giulio Oriani/Vega MG; 89 Sven Everaert (Architects: Claire Bataille & Paul Ibens); 91 (Architect: Misha Stefan); 92 Simon Upton/World of Interiors; 93 Mirjam Bleeker /Stylist: Frank Visser/Taverne Agency; 94 above Tom Mannion/World of Interiors; 94 below Marie-Pierre Morel/Stylist: Marie Kali/Marie Claire Maison; 96 above left Eric Morin; 96 above right Jean-Francois Jaussaud; 96 below Giorgio Possenti/ Vega MG; 97 Jan Baldwin; 99 James Mitchell/Red Cover; 100 above Guy Obijn; 100 below Fulham Kitchens; 101 Ken Hayden/Red Cover; 103 left Jake Fitzjones; 103 above right Jean-Marc Palisse/Madame Figaro (Designer:Aude Cardinale); 103 below right Eduardo Munzo/The Interior Archive; 104-105 Patrik Engquist (architect: Claessons, Koivisto + Rune); 106 above Stefan Muller-Naumann; 106 below Ken Hayden/Red Cover (Architect: John Pawson); 107 left David Sandison (Designer: Gail Hinkley); 107 right David Sandison (Architect: Gabriel Poole); 108 Eric Morin; 109 above Thomas Stewart/ IPC Syndication (Architect: Mooarc); 109 below left Maire-Pierre Morel/ Stylist:Puech & Postic/Marie Claire Maison; 109 below right Giorgio Possenti/Vega MG; 110-115 Winfried Heinze/Conran Octopus; 117 Lisa Linder/House & Garden/Condé Nast Publications Ltd (Designer: Olga Polizzi); 118 above Jennifer Cawley; 118 below Santi Caleca; 119 Verne Fotografie; 120-121 Grazia Branco/Iketrade; 121 above Patrik Engquist/ Architect: Erik Andersson & Magnus Ståhl); 121 below Deidi von Schaewen; 122 below left IMS Bildbyra; 122 below right Giorgio Possenti/Vega MG; 123 above Ricard Powers/Elle Decoration/stylist:Kate Ebben (Architect: Lara Gosling); 124 Giulio Oriani/Vega MG; 125 above Paul Ryan/International Interiors; 125 below Jan Verlinde; 126-127 Mirjam Bleeker/ Stylist: Frank Visser/Taverne Agency; 127 above Stellan Herner/ Stylist: Synnöve Mork; 127 below Ed Reeve/ The Interior Archive; 128 left Grazia Branco/Iketrade; 128 above right Andreas von Einsiedel/Red Cover; 128 below right Giorgio Possenti/Vega MG; 130-131 Michael Moran (Moneo Brock Architects); 133 James Morris/Axiom Photographic Agency (Architect: John Pawson); 134 left Jake Fitzjones/Red Cover; 134 right Guy Obijn; 135 left Per Gunnarsson/Stylist:Annelie Törngren; 135 right Jan Baldwin (Architect: Jonathan Clark); 137 above left Stellan Herner; 137 above right Verity Welstead/ Red Cover; 137 below Trevor Richards/ Abode; 138 Wayne Vincent/The Interior Archive; 139 left Giulio Oriani/Vega MG; 139 right Giorgio Possenti/Vega MG; 140 above Giorgio Possenti/Vega MG; 140 below left Alexander van Berge; 140 below centre Giulio Oriani/Vega MG; 140 below right Per Gunnarsson/ Stylist: Annette Ekjord; 142 left Peter Cook/View (Architect: Ludwig Mies Van Der Rohe); 142 right Eric Morin; 143 James Morris/Axiom Photographic Agency; 144 left Paul Grootes/ VTWonen/Sanoma Syndication; 144 right Chris Everard; 146 below Keith Collie (Architect: Azman Owen Architects); 146-147 Deidi von Schaewen; 147 right Richard Powers (Stephen Turvil Architects); 148 Peter Cook/View (Architect: Jonathan Woolf); 149 left Daniel Hertzell; 149 above right Guy Obijn; 149 below right Jake Fitzjones; 151 above left Deidi von Schaewen; 151 above right Nick Carter (ARK Architects); 151 below left Patrik Engquist/IMS Bildbyra; 151 below right Giulio Oriani/Vega MG; 152-153 Guy Obijn; 153 left Trevor Richards/Abode; 154 Marianna Wahlsten/Elle Decoration/ Stylist: Michelle Ogundehin; 155 above James Morris/Axiom Photographic Agency (Architect: Paxton Locker); 155 below left Jean-Francois Jaussaud; 155 below right Grazia Branco/Iketrade; 156 above left Neil Davis/Elizabeth Whiting & Associates; 156 below left Bulthaup; 156 right Taverne Agency; 158-161 Eduardo Munoz/The Interior Archive (Architect: Nico Rensch); 162 Graham Atkin-Hughes/Red Cover; 163 above Pere Peris/La Casa Marie Claire/Picture Press; 163 below left Winfried Heinze/ Red Cover; 163 below right Pere Peris/Picture Press/La Casa Marie Claire; 164-165 Guy Obijn; 165 above right Hotze Eisma/Stylist:Riane Landstra/Taverne Agency; 165 below right Richard Powers/Elle Decoration (Architect: Lara Gosling);166-169 Ray Main/Mainstream (Designer: Dominic Richards); 171 Winfried Heinze/Conran Octopus; 172 above Patrik Engquist; 172 below Winfried Heinze/Conran Octopus; 173 Daniel Hertzell; 174 Hotze Eisma/Taverne Agency; 176-177 Daniel Hertzell; 177 above Jan Baldwin; 177 below Steve Dalton/Red Cover; 178 left Ray Main/Mainstream (Designer: Andrew Martin); 178-179 Luke White/ The Interior Archive; 179 right James Morris/Axiom Photographic Agency (Architect:Claudio Silvestrin); 180 Alexander van Berge; 181 Hotze Eisma/ Taverne Agency; 182 above Chris Evans/Red Cover; 182 below left Per Gunnarsson/Stylist:Annelie Törngren; 182 below right Nick Carter; 184 left Ake E:son Lindman (Wingådhs Architects); ; 184 centre Simon Whitmore/Living etc/IPC Syndication; 184 right Mona Gundersen; 185 Paul Grootes/VT Wonen/Sanoma Syndication; 186 left Ray Main/ Mainstream; 186 right Richard Powers; 187 left Alexander van Berge; 187 right Dennis Brandsma/VT Wonen/Sanoma Syndication; 188 Eigen Huis & Interiors/Sanoma Syndication; 189 above Jake Fitzjones; 189 below Ray Main/Mainstream; 190 Alexander van Berge; 191 left Giulio Oriani/Vega MG; 191 right Robin Chanda (Stephen Turvil Architects); 192-194 Winfried Heinze/ Conran 196 left Solvi Dos Santos; 196 right Winfried Heinze/Conran Octopus; 197 Daniel Hertzell; 199 Winfried Heinze/Red Cover; 200 above Linda Hancock/Plain English; 200 below Ken Hayden/Red Cover; 201 left Guy Obijn; 201 right Rene Gonkel/Eigen Huis & Interiors/Sanoma Syndication; 202 left James Morris/Axiom Photographic Agency (Littman Goddard Hogarth Architects) ;202 right Deidi von Schaewen; 203 Hotze Eisma/Taverne Agency; 204 Daniel Hertzell; 205 Per Magnus Persson/Johnér Bildbyrå/ Photonica; 206 Daniel Hertzell; 207 Bulthaup; 209-224 Winfried Heinze/ Conran Octopus.

Pages 112/114 Painting by Mark Upton.

First published in 2002 by
Conran Octopus Limited
a part of Octopus Publishing Group
2–4 Heron Quays, London E14 4JP
www.conran-octopus.co.uk

Reprinted in 2002

Consultant editors: Elizabeth Wilhide, Lara Sargent
Publishing director: Lorraine Dickey
Senior editor: Muna Reyal

Creative director: Leslie Harrington, Lucy Gowans
Designer: Carl Hodson
Picture researcher: Clare Limpus
Special photography: Winfried Heinze
Styling for special photography: Sally Hayden, Sylvie Jones
Illustrator: Russell Bell

Production director: Zoe Fawcett, Adam Smith
Senior production controller: Manjit Sihra

British Library Cataloguing-in-Publication Data.
A catalogue record for this book is available from
the British Library.

ISBN 1 84091 233 2
Printed in China